The Poet, The Warrior, The Prophet

Dear Dan:

Here is an attempt
to say poetically
my poetic theology.

Sincerely,

Rubem A. Alves

THE POET,
THE WARRIOR,
THE PROPHET

The Edward Cadbury Lectures
1990

SCM PRESS
London

TRINITY PRESS INTERNATIONAL
Philadelphia

First published 1990

SCM Press
26–30 Tottenham Road
London N1 4BZ

Trinity Press International
3725 Chestnut Street
Philadelphia Pa. 19104

British Library Cataloguing in Publication Data
Alves, Rubem A. *1933–*
  The poet, the warrior, the prophet.
  1. Christian doctrine. God
  I. Title
  231

  ISBN 0–334–02475–7

Library of Congress Cataloging-in-Publication Data
Alves, Rubem A., 1933–
  The poet, the warrior, the prophet / Rubem A. Alves.
    p.   cm.
  ISBN 0–334–02475–7
  1. Creative ability—Religious aspects—Christianity.
  2. Christianity and literature.   3. Literature—Philosophy.
  I. Title.
  BT709.5.A48   1990
  230—dc20   90–39115

Typeset at The Spartan Press Ltd, Lymington, Hants
and printed in Great Britain by
Dotesios Ltd, Trowbridge, Wilts

To Wayne and Barbara

with whom I saw the running deer
in the twilight of Acadia

CONTENTS

LIST OF ILLUSTRATIONS

The illustrations by M. C. Escher (Collection Haags Gemeente-museum – The Hague) are reproduced by permission of M. C. Escher Heirs / Cordon Art, Baarn, Holland. The engraving by Albrecht Dürer is reproduced by permission of The Whitworth Art Gallery, University of Manchester.

Chapter I

UNLEARNING

But God chose what is foolish in the world,
even things that are not,
to bring to nothing things that are . . .

(I Cor. 1.27–28)

I try, therefore, to allow myself to be taken by the force
of all living life: forgetfulness . . .
There is an age when one teaches what one knows.
But there follows another when one teaches what one does not
  know . . .
It comes, maybe now, the age of another experience: that of
  unlearning . . .

Roland Barthes

From my chair I watch a spider which made her cobweb on the upper corner of the walls of my study. She was there yesterday and with a broom I got rid of it. Spiders and cobwebs are a sign of carelessness and I did not want my visitors disturbed by their annoying presence. But she returned and rebuilt her house in the same place. I believe that she has forgiven me and that she hopes that I will understand . . . I understand. And I decided to share my space with her.

The spider doubly fascinates me. First, because of what I see. There she is, safe and happy, over the empty space. There is no hesitation in her steps. Her legs move on the thin threads of her cobweb with tranquil precision, as if they were fingers of a violinist, dancing on the strings. Her cobweb: such a fragile structure, built with almost transparent gossamer. And yet it is perfect, symmetrical, beautiful, fit to its purpose. Second, because of what I do not see. I did not see her first move, the move which was the beginning of the web, the leap into the void . . . I imagine that tiny, almost invisible creature, hanging alone on the wall. She sees the other walls, far away, and measures the distance between them: an empty space . . . And there is one thing only she can count on for the incredible work she is about to start: a thread, still hidden inside her body. And then, suddenly, a leap into the void, and the spider's universe has began . . .

The spider: a metaphor of myself; I also want to weave a web over the void. But my world is not woven with anything material. It is made out of a substance more ethereal than gossamer thread, so ethereal that some have compared it to the wind: words. The human world is made with words. 'In the beginning, the Word . . .' And, like the spider's thread, words come also from within our bodies. Words are transformed flesh. I wonder if Nietzsche was not watching a spider when he said that 'man is a rope over an abyss' (*PN* 126).

[2]

The first word: a leap into the void, a leap out from the void . . .

But the spider is luckier than we are: she already has the recipe for such a portentous event: it was given to her by birth. Her body knows, her body remembers. But we have forgotten it. We do not know . . . As Eliot put it, we know 'words' but we are ignorant of 'the Word' (*CPP* 96).

I hear the 'Goldberg Variations'. They appear before me as a finished, solid word of art, all its parts forming a perfect structure. No loose threads, no unnecessary sounds. It is as it should be. Like the spider's web . . .

And yet there is a void of silence surrounding Bach's music, a void which is much greater than the void around the spider's cobweb. Indeed, the spider did not invent anything. She simply played again a motif which is being repeated, without variations, throughout millennia, by all spiders like her. When she leaped into the void, she already knew the score by heart; it was written in her body. But Bach's 'Variations' are a new word, never heard before. Bach had to hear them first, being played by a Stranger, in the silence of the inside of his body. They came, like the wind, the rope over the abyss, the loose threads of sound being braided into a single theme, and on it the musical cobweb was woven . . .

'Creatio ex nihilo' – out of nothing.

There are words which grow out of ten thousand things and words which grow out of other words: endless . . .

But there is a Word which emerges out of silence, the Word which is the beginning of the world.

This Word cannot be produced. It is neither a child of our hands or of our thoughts.

We have to wait in silence, till it makes itself heard: Advent . . . Grace.

When this Word is heard the whole body reverberates and we know that the mystery of our Being has spoken to us, out of its forgetfulness . . .

The French poet Mallarmé dreamed about writing a book with one single word. I thought he was crazy . . . But now, as I watch the spider, I think that I understand: he wanted to capture the first Word, which is the beginning of all others. This is the essence of poetry: back to the founding Word, which emerges out of the abyss of silence.

I used to be a good teacher. Like the spider, I knew how to weave my web of words. I knew what I taught. Even when I spoke without notes, and my students watched me weaving with the same amazement with which I watched the spider, the fact is that both of us, myself and the spider, were reading a text. Hers, thousands of years old. Mine, produced in my study. We read. We were 'lecturers'. Because this is the meaning of 'lecturing': to read words which were captured on paper, by the power of ink: the words come as birds in cages . . .

Good teachers, like the spider, know that lectures and webs cannot be woven in the void. They need foundations. Threads, no matter how light, no matter how thin, must be tied to solid things: trees, walls, beams. If the ties were cut, the cobweb is blown away by the wind, and the spider is homeless. Teachers know that the same is true of words: if they are separated from things they lose their meaning. Alone they do not stand. Like the cobweb, if their ties to solid things are cut, they become empty sounds: non-sense . . .

In order to avoid this danger good teachers make use of mirrors. If a word is a reflection, inside a mirror, of a reality outside, one can be sure that it cannot be non-sense . . .

Words: reflections . . .

The meaning of the image inside the glass is the real thing outside.

A good lecture: faithful reflections in a mirror.

A good teacher: a good mirror . . .

This metaphor is not mine. It was Nietzsche who spoke about the scientific ideal of the 'immaculate perception of all things'. But for this to happen, he added, one must 'lie prostrate before all things like a mirror with a hundred eyes' (*PN* 234).

Every word a faithful reflection:

[4]

to make visible and luminous the world which exists out there: to speak the truth, the whole truth, nothing but the truth.

For this to happen it is obvious that the mirror must be empty. A mirror with an inside (a crazy idea which one finds both in Carroll and Escher) is a liar. The mirror must be absent from itself. This is why, in rigorous scientific language, the word 'I' is never spoken. Instead of the 'I', the impersonal 'one'. One sees, one observes, one concludes. Who? Nobody. Everybody.

It happened, however, that my mirror got tired of this boring function of always repeating what is outside, and started having its own ideas. Instead of faithful reflections it began showing images for which there was no corresponding reality outside. Lewis Carroll could have been right. Mirrors may have an inside. And I could not resist the temptation of following Alice through the looking glass. And as I did it, another of my credentials as a respectable teacher was lost. I was no longer a mirror which could be trusted . . .

But there is more to be added. Normal spiders know, although unconsciously, what they have to do. They work with a method. I do not know if they learned from Descartes or if Descartes learned from them. The fact is that they start from solid and dependable foundations and proceed, step by step, according to a rational order. No improvisations are allowed. And they are never distracted by side tracks.

This is what is expected from a good lesson/lecture.

The teacher starts from what is known and proceeds methodically towards the unknown, building bridges with the materials at hand, constructing rigorous and cogent nets of words. The words march, one after another, like soldiers, in the direction determined beforehand.

As I went through the looking glass, however, I realized that inside the mirror words refuse to march. They do not obey the beat of the drum. They jump and dance as if they were in the midst of a choreographical spectacle. In the words of Octávio Paz, 'words collide with one another and produce metallic sparks or form phosphorescent pairs. The verbal firmament is filled with

new stars . . . Words and phrases emerge on the surface of language, still dripping humidity and silence between their cold scales'
(*AL* 42). In the psychoanalytical jargon, it is the 'free association
of ideas' . . . But would you trust your child to a dancing teacher?

A teacher gives lessons.

Lesson comes from 'lectio', a reading, from the Latin 'legere', to
read.

Lecture comes from 'lectura', and has the same meaning.

The teacher reads a written text; he gives a lesson; he delivers a
lecture.

The text: the words are immobilized on paper by the chemistry
of ink. When they made their first appearance they were not like
that: they were wild birds, flapping their wings . . . The teacher set
his traps, caught some of them and selected those which should be
locked with ink on the paper cage. Poor words . . . They have lost
their freedom. Now they are frozen in time and space. But later,
when the teacher begins his lecture, it will be his turn to lose his
freedom. He is now under the power of the written text. The
chemistry of ink keeps the words chained to the paper. But the
physics of light makes them fly from the paper to my eyes, and from
my eyes they come to my mouth, and I have to read them aloud. If,
by any chance, different birds pass by me flapping their wings, I
make believe I did not see them. If I feel tempted to fly along, the
text pulls me back and orders me to read what is written. Roland
Barthes, in his marvellous book on photography, remarks that
every photo is a photography of death. What we see is a time which
no longer is. The same thing can be said of a text. And we remember
the wisdom of the sacred texts: '. . . for the letter killeth, but the
Wind giveth life' (I Cor. 3.6).

This is the price one pays for security. Flying birds are unpredictable like the Wind: one does not know where they come from or
where they are going. Whenever they arrive they work havoc on
the order which had been carefully written on the text. It is obvious
that a prudent teacher will play with them at home but will be
careful to close the window in the classroom, lest he loses control
of the knowledge he is supposed to deliver.

But, for reasons unknown to me, I fell in love with the flying birds. Maybe because I began reading poetry . . . Maybe because I was seduced by psychoanalysis. The fact was that I became incapable of reading my lectures from the beginning to the end, because the wild birds broke through the windows and subverted the cartesian order of my thoughts. At the end, instead of having a clear, simple and cogent conclusion, what I had was a collection of fragments and a number of question marks . . . And I started asking myself if I was still a teacher, or if I had been converted to the ways of the Zen masters.

Teaching,
giving lessons,
delivering lectures:
reading.
Reading depends on the eyes.
And the eyes depend on light.
For one to read the lights must be on.
Indeed, one reads in order to make the lights shine.
The hearers must be en-lightened.
Obscurities must be clarified.
No dark corners . . .

Everything must be 'clear' and 'distinct', according to the classical rules of scientific etiquette, established by Descartes. If the lecturer is not clear enough, any one may demand 'clarification'. 'More light, please . . .'

Lecturing is explaining, explicating.

To explain: from the Latin 'ex-planare', to flatten, spread out, make level. A great bulldozer will push the mountains inside the abysses and everything will become a luminous plain under midday sun.

To explicate: from the Latin 'explicare', a verb derived from 'plicare' which means 'to fold'. To explicate: to eliminate all folds where darkness abides; to spread the text out, so that light will illuminate the whole surface.

A good teacher is a luminous creature. Wherever he goes darkness disappears. He even carries candles in his pockets, which he lights whenever he finds a dark corner on his text: footnotes . . .

I became sure that I was no longer a good teacher when, instead of turning the lights on, I preferred to turn them off . . .

Indeed, I love the mist which covers mountains and abysses, and I feel sorry when the sun dispels it because my imagination, together with elves and leprechauns, is deprived of the mist-eerie atmosphere without which it cannot breathe.

And I also love the darkness which abides inside the deep and lovely woods of Frost's poetry, and the light which fractures through unquiet waters in Eliot's poems, and the eerie atmosphere of the gothic cathedral, which reminds me of the entrails of the great fish inside the sea: a sunken cathedral . . . My whole Being reverberates, and I know that it belongs to the darkness of the woods, to the depth of the sea, to the mystery of the cathedral . . . If lights are turned on I am homeless . . .

I keep asking myself as to the reasons which led me astray and which force me to march in the opposite direction. But reasons I find none. Only suspicions . . .

I suspect that I do not want to decypher the mystery. I want questions and not answers. I want the sea and not the harbour.

I am unable to teach arrivals. I feel like Nietzsche who described himself as 'a departure at all gates' (*PN* 233). Instead of traps to catch birds, birds to catch traps . . . Answers are pregnant with questions. 'Always a beautiful answer who asks a more beautiful question', says E. E. Cummings (*SNL* 66). Like the Zen master who turns the question upside down with his koans. 'I only give answers to questions nobody asked', confessed Guimarães Rosa (*T*18). If his answers were answers to questions we had asked, we would have remained inside the very world from which the questions had emerged. Knowledge would simply confirm the sameness of the familiar world of our daily routines. Answers to make one stumble, answers which are the beginning of a new world.

I am not after conclusions. Conclusions are meant to shut (from the Latin 'con' plus 'claudere', to shut). The 'unconcluding' word, which opens the gates of the cages for the wild birds to fly again.

Every conclusion brings the thought process to a halt. As in Agatha Christie's books: once the murder is solved there is nothing left for one to think about. And it is useless to read the book again. When thought appears stabbed to death one may be sure that the murderer was a conclusion . . .

I remember, long time ago, I was fond of light. It happened, however, that by an accident, I became a friend to a poet. And I brought my texts for him to read. ' – Too much light', he remarked, as if his eyes had been hurt by clarity. 'Let's mix a bit of mist to your ideas, a bit of darkness to the argument, a bit of blurriness to the contours . . . Don't you know that a clear idea brings the conversation to a halt, whereas one unclear idea gives wings to the words and the conversation never ends?' Maybe this was the reason why Lessing said that, if God had offered him, in his right hand, the knowledge of the whole truth, and in his left, the perennial search for truth, with all the dangers and disappointments that this entails, he would opt for the left hand . . . (*CUP* 97). Lessing also loved more sailing across the ocean than arriving at the harbour. The 'thing' is neither at the point of departure or at the point of arrival, says Guimarães Rosa. It is in the 'going across' ('a coisa não está nem na partida e nem na chegada mas na travessia').

The pure joy of sailing,
the pure joy of thinking,
words flying with the Wind
for the sheer joy of flying . . .

I remember Saint Augustine. He remarked that there are some things which are to be enjoyed, and others which are to be used. 'To use something', he says, 'is to employ it in obtaining that which you love. To enjoy something is to cling to it with love for its own sake. Those things which are to be enjoyed make us blessed . . .' (*OCD* 9).

Words too, can be used as tools to lead us elsewhere. Bridges. Means to an end which is beyond them. Scaffolds which are dismounted, once the house is built. This is the way of science.

But words can be objects of enjoyment and we cling to them for the same reason that we cling to a sunset, to a sonata, to a fruit: for the sheer pleasure with which they are filled . . . Toys, ends in themselves . . . Words which are not to be understood, words which are to be eaten . . . The way of poetry.

And now I understand the metamorphosis I underwent: I no longer deal with words as 'things to be used'. I deal with them as 'things to be enjoyed'. I am no longer a teacher. I try to be a poet. My words are not addressed to the brain. They are addressed to the body. Words to be eaten . . . Every lecture is a dinner party, a eucharistic meal. 'Take, eat, drink, this is my body, this is my blood . . .' It seems that my place is not in the classroom, but in the kitchen. I deal with my words as the cook deals with the food he prepares . . .

Lectures as dinner parties . . .

Dinner parties take place under the rule of an etiquette. Etiquette is a series of rules, the purpose of which is to make sure that all the guests will be engaged in the same game. Etiquette is to eating what grammar is to speaking. It is useless to know the words if one does not know how to put them together. It is useless to have the food if the participants do not know how to go about eating. It is like dancing. The tune is not that important, provided that the pair knows how to move according to the rhythm. If the bodies follow the rhythm there will be harmony. If not, embarrassment . . .

In a delightful description of the etiquette for a dinner party in England, published in 1872 (*MEPP*), the author remarks that 'on each plate a bill of fare is placed, so that the guests may see what will be handed round'. One must know what one will eat, and it is assumed that all dishes must be to the taste of the guests. Otherwise the party could become an embarrassing digestive disturbance. The kind of food, the tastes, the spices, the smell, the colours – everything must be artfully combined for the pleasure of all. If the guest of honour is a vegetarian it is unforgivable to have beef as the main course. And also one should beware of offering pork to a rabbi. The choice of dishes reveals the host's soul, his knowledge about the taste of his guests . . .

But it is not enough that the food provokes your body. You must know how to eat. Gandhi, in his autobiography, tells of his embarrassment when he first came to England. He had never used forks, knives and spoons. His was the Indian etiquette: eating with one's fingers. Not to be able to skilfully use these tools is to confess that one does not belong to that world. So, he preferred the pain of hunger to the pain of being recognized as an outsider: during the whole trip he never went to the dining room. He ate crackers in his cabin . . .

A dinner party is not a simple occasion for eating. It has rules which must be obeyed. 'You should eat your soup from the *side* of your spoon, not take it from the point', says the etiquette expert. 'You should also make no noise in eating it; you should beware of tasting it while too hot, or swallowing it fast enough to make you cough.' Any breaking of the etiquette is a blunder which reveals that you were probably invited by mistake, since you don't belong there.

A dinner party is a magical ritual. Its purpose is to realize the dream of the alchemist: the universal transubstantiation of things. It starts with the magical powers of digestion. Onions, peppers, beans, potatoes, tomatoes, bread, beef, chicken, fish, lobsters, oysters, sweets, cheese, wine, beer . . . They are all different entities. They have different names. They have different properties. And yet, through the alchemic operations of the body they lose their identity. They cease to be what they were. They are assimilated. They become like the body (from the Latin 'assimilare', to make like; 'ad', to, and 'similis', like). They are incorporated: they become one with the body (Latin 'corpus', body). A meal is the triumph of the body over the food. All differences become sameness.

But another transformation takes place, when the etiquette is added to the food. Like in the sacrament: the real thing happens when words are added to bread and wine. Now the guests are transformed. True, they continue to be ambassadors, navy officers, professors, bankers, clergymen . . . But just as in a vegetable soup many different vegetables are cooked into one single broth, so the different guests become one single soup. They eat together, they become 'companions'. The meaning of this word is very suggestive. It comes from the Latin 'com', with, and 'panis', bread. Companions are those who eat bread together. The purpose of a dinner party is not the pragmatical end of nourishment and not only the pleasures of eating. It is hoped that eating together will become an occasion of companionship, friendship. The guests assimilate the food. The ritual assimilates the guests . . .

A lecture is a meal: words are distributed to be eaten. And like the dinner party, it also has an etiquette, a ritual.

A bill of fare must be also handed to the guests, so that they will know what kind of food is going to be served. If theirs is a different diet, if they belong to a group with divergent eating habits, they will have time to decline beforehand, thus avoiding the displeasure having to swallow what they abhor, only to vomit after the party is over. Lectures must have titles which announce the words which will be served.

Words will have to be well cooked, carefully prepared in advance, with due consideration for the eating habits of the guests. 'Never show your poem to a non-poet', a Zen saying advises. To serve a poem to a non-poet is like throwing pearls to the pigs . . . Words must be digestible. They also are to be assimilated, incorporated. The same alchemic operation which takes place at the dinner party must happen when a lecture is delivered: differences must become sameness. When differences become sameness the guests say: 'Yes, we understand . . .' 'Understanding' means: the words which were served are no longer strange entities. Now they have become what I am. I am the same. A new item has been added to my sameness. If this does not take place the cook-lecturer is frowned upon, and it is sure that the guests will no longer accept invitations for his dinner-lectures.

The etiquette of science. The first rule: we are to eat only words which are solidly rooted in things. The scientist is forbidden of simply enjoying the word, for the pleasure it delivers. Pleasure is, for him, something which spoils the whole meal. He does not trust the testimony of his body, the pleasure of his mouth, the joy of his nose . . . He checks the words in order to see if they are faithful reflections of the world outside. Indeed, this is what his diet is made of: the scientist eats reflections in the mirror. If the reflection is faithful he smiles and says: 'How good it tastes . . .' No, I am not inventing this. The basic rule of the etiquette of science you will find as the first statement of Popper's *The Logic of Scientific Discovery*: 'A scientist, whether a theorist or experimenter, puts forward statements, or systems of statements, and tests them step by step' (*LSD* 27). Popper says that the scientist 'tests' words, and not that he 'tastes' words. And testing is a thing of the mirror . . . And the purpose of the party, like the dinner, is to reduce differences to sameness. It is Thomas S. Kuhn who declares that 'normal science does not aim at novelties of fact or theory and, when successful, finds none' (*SSR* in *FUS* vol. 2, 114). If the apparent differences of fact were not reduced to the sameness of theory, all the guests would have a great indigestion . . .

Now, for a moment, let us play with our imagination. Imagination is the realm where thought is omnipotent and everything is possible. Let us imagine the impossible! A nightmare: a strange dinner, sheer non-sense, all the rules of reality turned upside down. The lobsters are alive, and so the fishes, the shrimps, the oysters, the fowl. The vegetables have knives and forks in their hands, and they are all sitting at the table, ready to begin eating the dinner. The hostess, a plumpy onion, orders the maid to bring in the entree. And there we are, just out of the oven, ready to be eaten. And right when the lobster is about to grab our nose with her claws we wake up in terror . . .

'Non-sense', we say with a sigh of relief . . .

Don't be too sure.

Dreams contain revelations of a repressed truth which can only appear under the mask of non-sense. It is in the non-sense the psychoanalysis looks for truth. And the gospel: wisdom in foolishness . . . 'Non-sense reflects in a split second the coherence

of the universal mystery which surrounds and creates us',
remarks Guimarães Rosa (*T* 8).

The reality which we familiarly know says: 'We eat the food;
we assimilate the food; the food becomes what we are.'

But suddenly a new truth is heard, when the etiquette is
subverted and the world is turned upside down:

'We are eaten by the food; the food assimilates us; we become
what we eat . . .'

The hostess offers me wine. The liquid is tame and innocent,
well behaved inside the glass. I take one sip, two, I empty the
glass. It is pleasant. The liquid is being assimilated into my body,
which feels the joy of the lightness of being. The world remains
the same, with just an extra drop of pleasure added to it.

But then, in a subtle moment, a reversal occurs. I no longer
drink the wine. It is the wine which drinks me. I have been 'drunk'
by it. I am drunk. Now it is not the wine which enters my body. It
is the wine which holds me inside a glass and drinks me, and I
enter into a totally different world, a strange world which I don't
know. My body is possessed by 'spirits' which had remained
outside till that moment. 'In vino veritas': in wine truth
abides . . .

Pentecost: they were filled with the Spirit. They spoke and
understood languages which had been unknown to them. And it
was as if they were drunk.

Pentecost is madness, non-sense, the breaking of the familiar
rules of understanding, the revelation of a knowledge which had
remained hidden. Wisdom emerges from foolishness. What we
call by the name of 'reality' is 'bewitchment'. 'The world must be
brought to a stop', D. Juan, the sorcerer, liked to say. (*JI* 13,14)
Otherwise it cannot be seen with different eyes. In Hegel's words,
'what is familiarly known is not really known, for the reason that
it is familiar' (*PM* 92). Truth appears when the world we
familiarly know is subverted, when its etiquette is no longer able
to maintain the farse. 'The truth', says Hegel, 'is the bacchanalian
revel, where not a member is sober' (*PM* 105).

A reversal of our eating habits.

Normality: we eat the food.
The reversal: we are eaten by the food.
Anthropophagy: the eucharist.
The eucharist is an anthropophagic dinner party: a magical ritual. One eats the body of the dead person in order to become like he was. One hopes to be eaten, assimilated by the food . . .
The eucharist: if the body and the blood were assimilated into our bodies, they would become what we are. But the eucharist is the reversal of normality: we eat and drink the bread and the wine, but it is the bread and the wine which eat us. We are to become what they are: the body and the blood of Christ.

To be drunk by the spirits,
to be eaten by the food:
a terrifying experience,
a nightmare,
madness . . .
The ego suddenly realizes that he is unable to keep his birds inside the cages.
He can no longer say: 'I have an idea . . .' because it is the idea which possesses him. One is no longer the master of the situation; one no longer knows what words will be spoken.
'I am very curious about what you are going to say,' someone said to Wilfried Bion, just before one of his conferences.
'Me too,' he replied . . .
Writers have known the magical power of words for a long time. Octávio Paz calls them 'voracious creatures'. E. E. Cummings suggests that they have the power to write, by themselves. 'When this book wrote itself,' he says (*SNL* 65). The book wrote itself? Was it not I who wrote it? As if the book had been written in regions far away from consciousness, emerging suddenly from its hiding place. Guimarães Rosa, the most disturbing of all Brazilian writers, says that his story 'The Third Margin of the River' came to him as he was walking in the street, just as the ball comes to the goal-keeper's hands. 'I just grabbed it and wrote it down as I arrived home', he said. But it is Nikos Kazantzakis who makes the description I like best of the magical power of the

words: '. . . letters of the alphabet frighten me terribly. They are sly, shameless demons – and dangerous! You open the inkwell, release them: they run off – and how you will ever get control of them again! They come to life, join, separate, ignore your commands, arrange themselves as they like on the paper – black, with tails and horns. You scream at them and implore them in vain: they do as they please . . .' (*DEBC* np).

The teacher is someone who made the trip and returned. He travelled over the unknown and wove his nets/nests. Now he speaks to those who did not go. He tells them how the world is. He shows them his cobwebs of words. He speaks and out of his words a map of the world is drawn, where one finds indications about the safe ways and about trails which lead nowhere.

Teaching is mapping the world, making it appear through the power of the word. 'My language denotes the limits of my world . . .' (*TLP* 115). Without maps life would be very difficult, the world would be permanently unknown, impossible to be learned.

The teacher carries his maps in his pocket. His birds are inside the cage. He is the master. He owns them. They are his possession. Like domestic animals which always return to where they belong: the dog which sniffs in the air the way back home, the carrier pigeon which flies to his owner, far away, the little ass in Guimarães Rosa's story which takes his drunk master amidst darkness and storm to the safety of his house . . . Yes, his words know the world. Everything is explained, everything is explicated . . .

The teacher is our good friend the spider. She knows. She is competent. She has a method. Her threads are tied to solid things. Her pupils, children, will learn the lesson. They will weave cobwebs over the void, also . . .

She faces life as a task, and she survives thanks to what she does. 'Justification by works . . .' Her being hangs on the threads she has herself produced out of her body . . .

But there are occasions when the safe, familiar world, comes to its end. Suddenly, the flat land of the ex-plained is interrupted by cliffs and canyons, and it is no longer possible to proceed . . . Or the smooth surface of the ex-plicated begins to crack and one realizes that what was believed to be a solid foundation was nothing more than frozen water, ice which begins to melt, as one's body sinks . . . Sometimes it is because we simply get tired of the safety and boredom of the dry land. 'The solidity of the dry land, monotonous, is a weak illusion. We want the illusions of the great sea, multiplied in its meshes of danger' (*FP* 104). And we sail to the unknown, obedient to the calling of our soul . . .

The Wind blows with unexpected violence.

The spider floats loose in the air.

There is nothing to be done. No one will be saved by works . . . Our encaged birds, our maps, our previous knowledge are of no avail.

We are at the end of the world.

We are at the beginning of the world.

We face the mystery.

We hear the Wind blowing, and yet we don't know where it comes from or where it is going.

We watch the flight of wild birds but they ignore the traps we had set for them.

In the words of D. Juan, the sorcerer, 'the world has stopped'. We no longer know. We are dumb, wordless.

There is nothing to be done but wait . . . Wait for an unknown Word to be spoken by the Unknown, a word which is heard only when our knowledge comes to an end, and which comes as an emissary of another strange world.

This is how I find myself, without maps, without encaged birds, without knowledge. I am no longer a teacher. I have no text to read, no lecture to deliver . . .

In my embarrassment I looked for friends, companions of ignorance. I was afraid of solitude. I began, then, to hear voices . . . I remembered E. E. Cummings who gave the title of 'Non-Lectures' to his six lectures delivered at Harvard. And I thought that this, indeed, could be the title of these 'conversations' – Tischrede, as Luther would have called them: non-lectures. My reading is a non-reading, my texts, pre-texts: empty word-cages with open doors, with the purpose of creating the void for the Word which cannot be said, but only heard. What matters is not what I say but the words that you hear, coming out of your forgotten depths.

I remembered also Wittgenstein, who understood philosophy as a battle against the 'bewitchment' which words can exert on us. Battle against words, for the sake of the only Word that matters: our truth. The spell must be broken, the bewitching word and the bewitched world must be forgotten . . . The dead must be buried, lest they return as ghosts which haunt the living ones . . .

Life demands forgetting . . .

And I remembered the words of Fernando Pessoa (Alberto Caeiro) who expressed my program much better and concisely than I could:

> I try to undress myself of what I have learned. I try to forget the mode of remembering they taught me, and scrape off the paint with which they painted my senses, to unpack my true emotions in order to be me (*PAlbC* 66).

One must forget in order to remember,
one must unlearn in order to learn anew . . .

This is, indeed, a strange theory of learning, a subversive philosophy of education which would horrify all respectable teachers and professors. I am ready to accept this strangeness and make mine Lichtenberg's words:

> I would like to become unfamiliar with everything
> in order to see again,
> to hear again,
> to feel again.
> Today one tries to spread knowledge everywhere; maybe, in a few centuries, there will be universities with the purpose of restoring the old ignorance . . . (*TR* 155).

But it was Roland Barthes who finally saved me from my embarrassment as a non-professor who delivers non-lectures and tries to teach forgetfulness. As I read him I knew that I was not alone and that, maybe, there was a bit of wisdom in my foolishness. These are the words with which he concluded his inaugural address as a professor of the College de France:

> I try, therefore, to allow myself to be taken by the force of all living life: forgetfulness . . .
>
> There is an age when one teaches what one knows.
>
> but there follows another when one teaches what one does not know . . .
>
> It comes, maybe now, the age of another experience: that of *unlearning*, when one allows oneself to be at the mercy of the imprevisible reworking which forgetfulness imposes on the sedimentation of all kinds of knowledge, of cultures, of beliefs . . . This experience has, I believe, an illustrious and old fashioned name, which I dare taking here without shame, at the very intersection of its etymology: *Sapientia*:
>
> no power,
>
> a bit of knowledge,
>
> a bit of wisdom,
>
> and the most of savor possible . . . (*L* 45–46)

I could not find better words to express my present truth. And I believe that they express the wisdom of the gospel:

One must be reborn, by the power of the unpredictable Wind, in order to enter the kingdom. One must become a child again . . .

Chapter II

SILENCE

What are we without the help of that which
does not exist?

Valéry

The nameless is the beginning of heaven and earth.
Darkness within darkness:
the gate to all mystery.

Tao Te Ching

There is a story.
I keep repeating it,
and every time I do wild birds pass by flying up high.
I first read it in one of Gabriel Garcia Marques' books. But this
happened a long time ago . . . I really don't know if the story I tell
is the same. Stories, indeed, are never the same, once retold. The
words may be the same, immobilized on paper. But every time
they are told they are different. Stories, like poems, are the same
which is always different . . .
It is about a village,
a fishermen's village,
lost in a nowhere/everywhere,
boredom mixed with the air,
each new day being like all the others,
the same empty words,
the same empty gestures,
the same empty faces,
the same empty bodies,
the excitement of love and life being something no / body
remembered . . .
It happened that on a day like all others a boy saw a strange
shape floating far away on the sea. And he cried. The whole
village came: in a place like that even a strange shape is an
occasion for excitement. And there they stayed, on the beach,
looking, waiting. Till the sea, slowly, no haste, brought the thing
and put it on the sand, to the disappointment of all.
A dead man.
All dead men are alike because there is one thing only to do with
them: they must be buried. In that village the usage was that the
women prepared the dead for burial. So, they carried the corpse to
a house, women inside, men outside. And the silence was great as
they cleaned it from the algae and the green things of the sea.

But suddenly a voice broke the silence: a woman . . .

'Had he lived among us he would have had to bend his head everytime he entered our houses. He is too tall . . .'

And they all nodded in approval.

Again the silence was deep. But another voice was heard. Another woman . . .

'I wonder about his voice . . . Was it like the whisper of the breeze? Like the thunder of the waves? Did he know that secret word which, once uttered makes a woman pick up a flower and stick it in her hair?'

And they all smiled.

Silence again. And again, the voice of another woman:

'These hands . . . How big they are! What did they do? Did they play with children? Did they sail through the seas? Did they fight many battles? Did they build houses? Did they know how to caress and to embrace a woman's body?'

And they all laughed,

and were surprised as they realized that the funeral had become resurrection: a movement in their flesh, dreams, long believed to be dead, returning, ashes becoming fire, forbidden desires emerging to the surface of their skins, their bodies alive again . . .

Their husbands, outside, watched what was happening to their wives, and they were jealous of the drowned man, as they realized that he had a power which they themselves did not have. And they thought about the dreams they had never had, the poems they had never written, the seas they had never seen, the women they had never loved.

The story ends by telling that they finally buried the dead man.

But the village was never the same.

Did you understand the story?

I hope not.

If you did it is because you have succeeded in digesting it.

But stories are like poems; they are not to be understood.

Something which is understood is never repeated.

Understanding exhausts the word. It leaves the word empty with nothing left to be said. Once the word is understood it is reduced to silence.

But a story is like a sonata, a love embrace, a poem, a sunset: we want them to be repeated, because their savor is inexhaustible. They look like cages; they are built with word-bars. But they are empty: the Void is always there, never to be filled.

A funeral: what an exacting etiquette! Even death has its rules . . . All the mourners know what is expected from them. They know the proper words, the proper gestures. Decomposition must be cooked properly, according to recipes all agree upon, so as to become palatable and digestible.

Many burials had occurred before in that village, and there was no memory of any occasion in which the accepted rules of propriety had been broken. Each corpse is a firm foundation for the spiders to tie their threads around: each corpse is the beginning of a long conversation. The dead have names, and around each name many stories can be told. Corpses are all covered with signs. They are texts. They can be read: lessons, lectures . . .

'Do you remember?', the mourners ask.

And the weaving begins . . .

One has always what to talk about before the dead.

And so, the etiquette of death makes sure that there is no interruption in the etiquette of life.

But that dead man . . . He had no name, no history . . .

He was no place for the spiders to tie their threads around.

They did not know what to do before that enormous void. The silence round it was absolute. And the abyss, unfathomable.

It is true that he was covered with signs. But they were all written in a language nobody knew.

His death was different: it closed all the normal ways of speech. The etiquette was of no avail. They did not have an object to talk about.

He was an empty cage.

[24]

The world was stopped.

In common burials the living ones are in charge. But now the situation is reversed: the dead man presides over the liturgy with the mystery of his silence . . . Who is more disturbing: the silent guest who does not say one single word, or the one who says too many words?

Mystics and poets have known that silence is our original home . . .

The *Tao Te Ching* says that 'the named is the mother of ten thousand things', the familiar world of our daily lives, but 'the nameless is the beginning of heaven and earth'. Before the Word, the Void. 'And the earth was without form and void, there was darkness upon the face of the abyss, and the Wind of God moved over the face of the waters' (Gen. 1.2). 'Word, I don't care about this common place', says Adélia Prado. 'What I want is the magnificent chaos from which it emerges, the dark places where it is born' (*B* 30).

We speak words in order not to hear the Word which comes out of silence. Too many words to exorcize the Word. 'Silence', says Octávio Paz, 'this lake with a smooth and compact surface in whose depths, submerged, words are waiting' (*AL* 179). There is a Word which can be heard only when all words have become dumb, an eschatological Word which makes itself heard at the end of the world. Pure grace, no encaged bird, a wild bird which flies with the Wind . . .

The dead man: behind him the silence and mystery of the sea. The sea: maybe this is our original dwelling place. 'Our gaze is submarine', says Eliot. 'Our eyes look upward and see the light which fractures through unquiet waters . . .' (*CPP* 112). And it seems that Cecilia Meireles lived in the same world:

'But in this mirror,
in the depth of this cold marine light,
my eyes, two dim fishes,
swim, looking for myself . . .' (*FP* 81).

And it is from inside the belly of the great fish that Jonah remembers his forgotten word. And he prays . . . (Jonah 2.1, 5).

If not the sea, the silence which abides in the deep darkness of the woods, as in Frost's poem:

> The woods are lovely, dark and deep.
> But I have promises to keep,
> and miles to go before I sleep . . .

Would it be a simple coincidence – that poets keep speaking about the same worlds? Or could it be that they live in the mystery where our Being abides? Poetry: this desperate attempt to say what cannot be said.

Silence: the Void where unthinkable creatures live, protected by darkness.

The Void.

The *Tao Te Ching* says in its verse eleven:

> Thirty spokes share the wheels hub;
> but it is the center hole which makes it useful.
> Shape clay into a vessel;
> but it is the space within that makes it useful (*TTC* 11).

We are the wheel,
we are the vessel.
Our soul is a Void . . .

Is not the Void God's dwelling place? 'Our Father who art in heaven . . .' When I was a boy and I repeated these words, I thought about a far away place, filled with angels and glittering buildings. But it did not attract me a bit. But just a few verses ahead the same word is used to point to the house of the birds: 'Look at the birds of the air . . .' (Matt. 6.26). Strange: the same word *ouranos* is translated in two different ways. Were the translators afraid of saying that God was like the birds, that they all needed the empty space? The birds, to fly; God, to blow like the Wind . . .

The wheel can be of help only because of the Void which lies in its heart. The vessel can hold water only because it is a gracious emptiness.

Thought demands the Void for the unpredictable to come in . . . Something which was known to those who built the Gothic cathedrals: the walls, the engravings, the sculptures, the stained glasses – all of them were built in order to bring an empty space into being.

'To think', says Octávio Paz, 'is to produce the Void for Being to emerge' (*AL* 126).

Being lies submerged.

Where?

Hidden by the reflecting surface of the lake,
in the depths of water.

Overspoken by the rattling of ten thousand words,
in the spaces of forgetfulness, where they cannot be heard.

Blinded by the glare of midday sun,
In the darkness of night.

There they were, without words to say, around the dead man. It was as if one could hear Rilke's words in the air:

> Hear this constant message
> which generates silence . . . (ED 5)

But suddenly, out of silence, strange words began to be heard.

Forgotten . . . The villagers had lost all memory of them: they had been dead for a long time . . . But no. They had only hidden themselves away from the rattle of the ten thousands words. Indeed, they cannot be spoken at the same time: they belong to different worlds. Some are creatures of light, they are heard when we are awake, at day time, and abide by the reflexes which shine on the surface of the lake. They are many. But some are mysterious entities which live hidden in submarine depths or in the darkness of the woods. Being shy – or forbidden – they move out of their hiding place at night, when we sleep and dream. Most of the time they are heard but not understood, as if they had been spoken in a foreign language. They are not many. And poets and mystics have even said that they are one single Word: a Word which contains a universe.

No wonder that these strange words are not admitted in our dinner parties and lectures. Truth, thus says our etiquette, is a creature of light and understanding. 'Cogito, ergo sum': I think, therefore I am. My being abides in light, together with clear and distinct ideas. Truth is a faithful reflection inside the mirror. And for reflections to exist, the lights must be on. And now one speaks about words which abide in darkness and silence . . .

The Greeks knew that truth abides in darkness: those who see are blind, and only the blind can see. And those who have good eyes or are sober cannot see it. Oedipus had a brilliant mind. He was able to unravel the riddles which abide in daylight. And he killed the Sphinx, as he gave the right answer to her question. But his own truth remained hidden . . . Only those who moved in darkness were able to see the hidden tragedy which lurked behind his light. First, a man who got drunk, in a banquet: he told Oedipus that his parents were not his parents. Then, the oracle of Delphi, 'who always spoke the truth, never gave straight answers, in the upright Protestant way; he always spoke in riddles . . . Ambiguities . . . To teach is not to tell, is not-to-tell; like Heraclitus, the obscure . . .' (*LB 245*). And finally the seer Teiresias, 'whose soul grasps all things, the lore that may be told and the unspeakable, the secrets of heaven and the low things of earth' – these are Oedipus words. And yet, he was blind. He did not see with his eyes, because he saw with his soul. *Oedipus Rex* is a story about those who, having eyes, do not see, and those who, being blind, see. Truth is beyond the visible. But it is also beyond the audible: it is ab-surd (Latin: 'ab' plus 'surdus', deaf), unworthy of being heard: this is why its admittance is forbidden by the rules of etiquette. Truth is forced to remain outside the room where the banquet is being held, in the corridors and outside patios, under the protection of the shadows. Truth is underground, repressed, it moves away from any evidence. For one to see it one must close one's eyes; for one to say it one must close one's mouth: this is the original sense of mystery: 'closing the eyes' or 'closing the mouth' (*ST* vol. I, 108).

Psychoanalysis was born when it was realized that words are

full of silence. Those who only hear and see what is said and written understand nothing: the letter kills . . . The body speaks in tongues. Babel must be overcome by Pentecost. Truth lives on the reverse side of what is familiarly known. Wisdom is foolishness, foolishness is wisdom. Like the 'Deus Absconditus', truth also comes hidden, under a disguise. It wears masks. All words, taken literally, are false. Truth lives inside the silence which is around the words. One must pay attention to what is not said: to read between the lines. Floating attention: it touches the words, without falling into their trap. Lest one is bewitched by them . . . Beware of the seduction of clarity! Beware of the deceit of the obvious! The daylight truth was that the man was dead. What was obvious was that his corpse was full of silence. And yet, the thoughts of the villagers danced . . . Somehow they experienced what César Vallejo said:

'. . . su cadáver estava lleno de mundo',
his dead body was full of worlds (*AL* 116).

Psychoanalysis is an attentive hearing of the silence which lies in the interstices of words, in order to hear what was not spoken.

But this was not psychoanalysis invention: psychoanalysis only payed attention to something which had been known for millennia, but later swept out of the illuminated room as dirt, by the triumphant etiquette of clear and distinct ideas.

Long before psychoanalysis, the poets. Poets, they all look for the words which only grow out of silence.

Poetry: diving into the mysterious lake, moving through the looking glass, away from the deceptive surface of reflections, into the depth where the words are born and live . . .

'What you think and feel, this is not poetry, yet', says Carlos Drummond de Andrade, the greatest of the Brazilian poets.

Enter silently into the world of words:
there live the poems which wait to be written.
They are paralysed, but there is no despair . . .
Get closer; contemplate the words . . .

Each has one thousand secret faces under the neutral face.
And they ask: 'Have you brought the key?'
They took refuge in the night, the words . . .
Still wet and sleepy,
they roll in a difficult river . . . (*RD* 76ff.).

Silence is the space where words come to life and begin to move. Once they existed because we uttered them. They depended on our will to think, to speak, to write: tame birds in our cages. But in silence a metamorphosis occurs. They become wild, free. They take the initiative. And we can only see and hear. They come to us from beyond. And we find ourselves in another world, a world the beginning of which is the Word. Common places become transparent and one can see thousands of meanings and chaos, on the reverse side. A world we had not visited before. No, maybe we visited it . . . Maybe we were born in it . . . But it was forgotten, when the glare of the reflections made us oblivious of our origins. Every poem is a testimony of this lost world. This is why its words are creatures of depth, still 'dripping humidity and silence between their cold scales' (*AL* 42).

What poets have seen and want to say cannot be said. Goethe knew that the task of poetry is impossible, because it is 'the language of the unspeakable' (*LV* 15).

The dead man did not say one single word.
He was full of silence.
And his silence was the space of remembrance.
His dead body was full of their lost memories . . .
He was a poem . . .
Clarity brings thought to a halt.
But in darkness the world is born.

Chinese art: have you noticed that its landscapes are always covered with clouds and mist? They are there because the soul needs them . . . During the cultural revolution, however, the mists were forbidden. Revolutions are times of certainties. No hazy scenaries, no privacy. Full luminosity to scare the dreams away. Because dreams are testimonies that the soul has not become an encaged bird. Orwell perceived clearly that in a totalitarian state dreaming is a crime. Instead of dreams, realism. No dark corners, no shadows, no mystery. Total visibility. The contours must be clearly drawn, lest one may be seduced to allow heretical thoughts to come in. Meanings are clearly stated, with no intervals in their interstices. And one thinks that the ideal of communication has been achieved. The ideal teacher, the perfect lecturer. But total visibility is totalitarian: it fills the inner spaces of the soul with images which come from outside, and the truth which dwells inside is forced to remain unspoken. In the psychoanalytical language: repression. Total visibility puts the soul at the mercy of the eyes. Eyes are persecuting entities. Cruel gods have their eyes always open, and no eyelids: they are never shut, they are never asleep. Clouds and mists, on the contrary, are generous: they are a refusal to show and say: they open an empty space of silence . . . The bashful creatures which live inside our forests and seas appear then, protected by the shadows.

'What did the painter want to say?'

The answer is easy, if one is before a realistic painting. But if there are clouds and mists, what I see is my own face: the scenaries which abide inside my flesh.

I am a psychoanalyst. In my office I have two pictures. One of them is a luminous landscape, with bright colours, red poppies on a green prairie, and at the end blue mountains touching the skies. When people see it for the first time they usually say the same words:

'How beautiful it is!'

But that is all. Clarity says everything which is to be said. The conversation is brought to an end. The soul is possessed by ten thousand things.

The other is a dark and deep forest, hazy shapes, indefinite trees, a lonely trail which disappears in an eerie atmosphere of diffuse mist. Everything suggests mist-eerie . . . When people see it they stop: they do not know what to say. But after some moments of indecision, the same question:

'I wonder . . . What is it which is hidden by the mist, behind the trees, in the dark?'

This picture: a poem; it does not intend to say what it shows. The visible is only the discrete border which suggests the invisible, the nameless, that which cannot be said. The eyes which only see the visible do not see the absence which is there.

A dream . . . Truth is hidden. It is absent. It is not shown, it is not said. It is only evoked . . . In this dark, silent space, strange creatures begin to move: absences, only visible with the eyes of desire and love . . .

'Get nothingness back into words', says Norman O. Brown. 'The aim is words with nothing to them; words that point beyond themselves rather than to themselves; transparencies, empty words. Empty words, corresponding to the void in things' (*LB* 259). Reverberations from Kierkegaard, who perceived that truth is essentially a secret (*CUP* 73). Not the kind of accidental secret which is secret only because it has not yet been revealed as word. Secret because no word can say it. The word is only the edge of the abyss. The abyss, itself, is clouded with mist, surrounded by silence. The ten thousand words which communicate the knowledge of the ten thousand things are useless: the wind cannot be caught with nets, the beauty of the deep and dark woods vanishes in the air if lanterns are lit. A word is then heard: a word which is not knowledge, a word which is not a cage for wild birds. It says without saying, like a work of art; it evokes, like poetry; and, as a fish that one wants to catch with one's bare hands, it elusively escapes from our control.

Christology: a poem is recited before the Void.

'The teaching about Christ begins with silence', says Bonhoeffer in the first line of his Christology (*WWJC* 9). And I imagine that a new prologue for the gospel of John could be written:

> 'Before all things existed
> there was a great pregnant silence.
> And then, suddenly,
> "ex nihilo",

a Word was heard,
and the world began.'
'Ex nihilo' out of the Void . . .
The Void is full of worlds,
like the corpse of the dead man . . .
The name of the dead man: was it Jesus Christ?
The villagers, women and men, began to speak.
Nothing about the dead man.
Out of him.
Because of his silence.
Their speech was not an original act.
They spoke because they heard.
They heard words which were unknown to them:
words which were not found in their stock of familiar
knowledge.
Their caged birds had no songs for the occasion.
Wild birds, coming from forgotten regions –
they did not even know that they existed! –
flapped their wings, feathers of bright colours,
singing songs unknown,
possessed their souls and bodies,
and they spoke –
like poets,
like magicians,
like lovers,
like theologians,
because theology is the Word which is spoken before the
Void,
as an invocation of the Absent . . .
We dwell in forgetfulness.
The words we know are not our truth.
I think, therefore I am.
I am where I think.
But now the world is reversed.
Where I think, there I am not.
I am where I do not think.

I am where there is forgetfulness.
'We do not even know how to pray'.

Prayer: the name of our desire But it is precisely the name of our
desire that we no longer know. We have lost the map which leads
us back to the house of our Being, paradise.

We have forgotten how to speak: signs which are too deep for
words, inarticulate groans (Rom. 8.26).

But it does not matter if we don't remember because there is a
Stranger who dwells in us who knows what our forgetfulness
says . . .

There, under the reflections on the surface of the lake,
there where clear and distinct ideas abandon us,
there where our gaze is submarine,
the Spirit says its mysterious Word.

And God – in spite of our forgetfulness – 'knows what is being
said in that language we do not understand'.

Our truth abides beyond our knowledge. It abides in our
dreams.

The villagers could not say anything about the dead man: he
did not have a name . . .

And yet, it is out of this silence that new words are heard.

His silence made them dream again:
had he lived in our village,
had we heard his voice,
had we been touched by his hands . . .

It seemed that they were telling stories about the dead man. But
how could they, if they knew nothing about him? The stories they
told about the dead man were stories about themselves: their
dreams being resurrected from the graveyard where they had
been buried. Their soul was the graveyard . . .

Now their bodies were resurrected. They were alive again. Their
soul returned to their flesh. They were dreams made flesh . . .

And they discovered that they all had the same dreams. They all
participated in the same eucharistic festival. The beginning of a
community: when the many have the same dreams.

'Con-spirers': they breathed the same air. We breathe the same absence: dreams are emissaries of the absent . . .

Every word was a confession:

'Hoc est corpus meum. This is the bit of my flesh which became alive again by the power of the silence of this dead man . . .'

The memory of the forgotten desire possessed their bodies. And they were resurrected for life.

Isn't this strange?

Dreaming comes from desire, and desire is longing. But longing exists only before the Void . . .

They were resurrected because they were possessed by the power of the Void.

Which makes us remember Valéry's words:

> What are we without the help of that which does not exist? (O 966).

Chapter III

WORDS AND FLESH

The old pond –
a frog leaps in,
And a splash.
                    Basho

Woe to those who did not bite the dream
and of whose foolishness
not even death will redeem them.
                    Paulo Leminski

Could I take along with me, to the other world,
the dreams that I forgot to dream?
These dreams – the dreams that I did not dream –
they are the corpse.
                    Alvaro de Campos

And the village was never the same . . .

The dead were resurrected.

How can we account for this miracle?

The story is silent . . . It tells, without offering any kind of explanation. It shows the surface of the lake where the ten thousand reflections played their game of deception. And it says that suddenly a stone, coming from nowhere, was cast into the lake . . . Like the old story about an angel who, from time to time, would trouble the waters of the pool (John 5.4). And it describes how magic fishes, coming from its depths suddenly jumped out of the water, and those who saw them were healed.

The story is surrounded by darkness. The story is to us what the dead man was to the villagers: a mystery . . .

Darkness is indeed needed: magical powers are afraid of too much light. They are like love, which demands discretion, dim lights, unspoken words. One does not make love under the light of midday sun. It is not possible to seduce with the help of scientific concepts. Seduction speaks the language of poetry. The 'lovely, dark and deep' shadows of the woods are more cosy. It is there that imagination awakes from its slumber. And imagination is needed if magic is to take place, because, as Feuerbach once said, 'the power of the miracle is the power of imagination' (*EC* 130).

An outsider would not have noticed any visible changes. The same skies, the same sea, the same faces . . . But they knew that everything was different. Their banal everyday life which they knew with such familiarity had been transfigured. They had been given new eyes and the solid objects and stone faces which filled their space became transparent. It was as if they saw invisible things which were visible only to those who had seen the angel troubling the waters of the pool – the dead man. Do you remember Dali's 'The Last Supper'? The Son of God – the farewell signs already visible on his face – is in the upper room with his disciples. Light filters through everything: through Christ's body, through the glassy walls . . . And through this magical transparency the whole world and the cosmic spaces become iridescent and are embraced by the outstretched arms of a man . . . The world will never be the same again . . .

By looking at the smiling faces of the villagers one has the feeling that they must have seen something beautiful . . .

Was it the dead man's face? It could not be, because death is always ugly. When a mourner smiles at a dead body it is not because of what is seen, but because of what is no longer there, the memory of a beauty which once was but no longer is . . .

Because of themselves? I suspect that, in that village, all mirrors had been broken, for fear; all of them already had the image of death inside their eyes, and it is likely that it was there that Escher had the inspiration for his drawing 'Eye' . . . Death dwells in mirrors. They are the place where Death can be seen closest to us, slowly spreading its presence over our bodies, taking possession of the flesh which will be hers, one day.

Where did they see the beauty which made their faces shine?

Had they a magic mirror with powers to see things which are invisible to the eyes?

Yes, they did . . .

They dreamed. And dreams are mirrors of the invisible . . .

Normal mirrors reflect things which are present; but dreams show things which are absent.

Did you know that images have the power to possess those who see them? Riobaldo, Guimarães Rosa's mythical hero, says that it takes just one minute to transform a chickenhearted person into a brave one: it is enough to look in the mirror with the face of a brave one . . . (*GSV* 38).

The villagers, in their dreams, saw themselves as winged entities
and their bodies began to fly.

They were possessed by the vision of their dormant beauty.

The stories they told about the dead man were not about him.

How could they tell stories about someone they had never seen before?

Their stories about the dead man were stories about themselves. Stories not about what they were (this was what they saw when they looked in their mirrors . . .), but stories about what they desired to be: this is what they saw as they faced their dreams . . .

Inside our flesh, and mixed with the noises of Death, there is written an indelible story of beauty. And even without knowing we know that we are destined to this happiness: the Prince must meet the Sleeping Beauty.

The villagers remembered. Their stories were the return of a lost time: the past, desired, repressed, forgotten, dead, resurrected from the grave.

Did it really happen?

Had they been really beautiful, somewhere in the past? Did they see in the magic mirror of their dreams a face as it had actually been, once?

Once?

When was that?

'Once upon a time' – thus begin all children's stories.

My daughter, when she was a small girl, always wanted to know if the story I was about to tell had actually taken place. And I found it difficult to explain. As I told you, explanations destroy the magical power of the words. How could I explain to her that the story was always happening in the present just because it had never happened in the past, in the far distant land? The best that I could say was: 'I don't know . . .'

Stories are like music. One does not ask of Brahms' 'First Symphony': 'Did it ever happen?' No, it did not. The symphony is not a portrait of something which happened 'apax', once and for all. That which happened once and for all is forever lost. The symphony: everytime it is played its magic happens again. The beautiful wants to return . . . Its time is sacred; it is reborn every morning; it is the time of resurrection. But chronological time is the time which devours its children, it is the time of the 'never more', the time of mourning without remedy, the time of death.

'Once upon a time, in a far distant land . . .': a cloud of mist covers the narrative to conceal its real time and space which are 'now' and 'here'. Mythical past is always present: in the depths of the lake there is no time. The 'once upon a time in a far distant land' is a metaphorical way of speaking about a present loss. The story draws the contours of the abyss which lies inside our bodies; its words are the cobweb over the void . . . 'Words and sounds, are they not rainbows and ellusive bridges between things which are eternally apart?' (*PN* 329), asks Nietzsche.

Beauty is the name of what we have lost.

And what we have lost makes itself present as longing and desire . . .

This is why it never appears on the surface of the lake. There is the dwelling place of the presences, the objects we have, and yet longing remains. Beauty appears in another mirror which lives inside our bodies. Its name is imagination. In imagination things which do not exist allow themselves to be seen.

'The finger points to the moon'; thus starts a Zen saying. The eyes move from the finger to the moon – and they see. But if the skies are clouded, if there is no moon to be seen, then the finger will not do. The eyes will turn to the cloudy skies, but they will not see anything.

'Moon' – someone says.

And the moon shines inside the soul, even if it is absent from the skies . . .

Inside our bodies, there dwell the absent moons. And the word has the power to make them visible to the soul.

'In hope we are saved; now to hope is not to see . . .'

The body: a thin web of flesh woven over the abyss of beauty, the only evidence we have for it being the word.

Everytime the story is retold,
> the words are recited,
> the melody is replayed,
> the myth is repeated

we are back in our foundations: the flesh trembles as it hears the sounds which invoke the images of its lost beauty. Octávio Paz describes this magical experience:

> Everyday we cross the same street or the same garden; every afternoon our eyes meet the same red wall, built with bricks and urban time. Suddenly, in a day like all others, the street leads to another world, the garden has just been planted, the tired wall is covered with signs. We had never seen them, and now we are surprised because they are so overwhelmingly real. Their compact reality makes us doubt: are the things like that or otherwise? No, this that we are seeing for the first time we had already seen before. Somewhere, where we had never been before, the street, the garden, the wall already were. And surprise follows nostalgia. It seems that we remember, and we would like to return to that place, where things are always like that, bathed in a very old light which has just been born. We belong there. A gust of wind blows on our face. We are spellbound, suspended in the middle of the immobile afternoon. We realize that we belong to another world. It is the previous life which returns. (*AL* 161)

Once upon a time,
in the beginning,
a story was told,
a word was heard . . . (John 1).

The word was spoken to those who had it written on their bodies: its home. But it sounded like 'a noisy gong or a clanging cymbal . . .' The flesh remained cold, unmoved. It did not understand it, although it was its mother tongue . . .

But some remembered . . .

Some felt their bodies trembling . . .

They recognized the name . . .

Just the name? Is that enough?

What about his teaching? What about his life? What about his wisdom?

Names engraved on the bark of old trees: for me they mean nothing. But I can imagine that someone could cry, just at the sight of them: the one who wrote them, long ago. The name contains everything which needs to be remembered: images of a lost happiness. Maybe Mallarmé's book has been already written many times, on the bark of old trees . . .

Names are more than reflections inside a mirror. They are sacred. 'Hallowed be thy name . . .' Paul Lehmann proposes a pregnant translation for the second commandment: 'Thou shall not utter the name of God as if this uttering made no difference . . .' Names are magical entities, filled with power.

Names: rainbows and bridges over this great void which has the name God.

When the name is remembered, resurrection begins.

Not the dead man's name but their own names:

'His dead body was full of names, like God . . .'

The mystery of love: we love not the thing but the words which are written in it. We are beautiful because of the poems that our flesh knows by heart, even without remembering them . . .

It was fall in the state of Maine. They told me that the colours had been especially bright that year. The beauty was so great that it hurt: the last explosion of colours before the arrival of winter. It was the apple season. On the centre table of my small apartment, a basket full of red apples. My students around me.

'– We love not the thing, but the words which are written in it', I said.

One of the students looked at me, picked up an apple, gave it a bite, and said:

'I love apples . . .'

The juice dripped from the sides of his mouth as he smiled at me. I understood what he was saying without words:

'An apple is an apple: this round, red, juicy fruit. When I bite an apple I bite its flesh only . . . No words . . .'

I took the apple from his hands, the same fruit, gave another bite and said:

'– I love apples, too. But we can never eat the same fruit, even if the thing is the same. This very apple belongs to two different worlds. Yours is filled with memories of past falls; there are yellow and red leaves in it; and even a chilly breeze. I even see Robert Frost's face:

> O hushed October morning mild,
> Thy leaves have ripened to the fall . . .
> Tomorrow's wind, if it will,
> Shall waste them all . . .

Don't you see the colours, don't you hear the noise of the leaves, as you walk on them, don't you have goose pimples, as the breeze touches your skin?

But around my apple there circles another universe you will never know . . . I was a boy in a small town in Brazil. Apples did not grow there. I had never seen one. The name I knew, and also pictures, from Snow White's story. I knew that they grew in distant lands and that, if they were to come to where I lived, they would have to travel a long way. My father had returned from a trip and brought me presents, of which I have no memory. Except for an apple. It came wrapped in a silky, yellow paper. I did not have courage to eat it, because if I ate it, I would lose it. And I dreamed that I was the only boy in that town to have a magical fruit. So, I kept polishing its shiny skin as a way of postponing its inevitable end. Yes, I love apples . . . But, as you see, yours and mine, although they are the same, contain different universes. They tell different stories . . .'

Do you remember the Little Prince? He had seduced the Fox, at her request. And she fell in love with him. But the farewell time arrived and the Little Prince announced that he had to go.

'I am going to cry', said the Fox.

'I am not to be blamed for it', the Prince apologized. 'I did not want to seduce you. Now you are going to cry. What was the good that falling in love did to you?'

'I did me good because of the wheat fields . . .'

'The wheat fields?', the Prince asked.

'Yes', the Fox replied. 'I am a Fox, and as you know foxes do not eat wheat. We eat chickens. But your hair is blond and the wheat fields are golden. From now on everytime the wind blows over the wheat fields I will remember you . . .'

Theologians used to define a sacrament as the 'visible sign of an invisible grace'. The wheat fields ceased to be wheat fields. They became something else: rainbows and bridges over things eternally apart. Poetic metaphors: visible signs of an invisible grace. Now the wheat field abandons the realm of agriculture and enters the realm of poetry. It is a metaphor. 'This is that': the wind blows over the field and I hear your voice: a bit of longing, a bit of beauty, a bit of sadness. One flies over the abyss. Ecstasis: one is no longer there . . . This is love. 'I have told you that metaphors are dangerous', says Milan Kundera. 'Love begins by the power of a metaphor. Love begins in the moment when a woman is inscribed with a word in our poetic memory' (*ILS* 210).

That the wheat fields have the power to perform this magical operation is understandable, because they are beautiful. But who could imagine that the repulsive fish-cleaning operation in the kitchen could become a sacrament for love-making in the bedroom? Listen to this poem by Adélia Prado:

There are women who say: 'My husband may fish,
if he wishes,
but he will have to clean the fishes.
Not me. At any time of the night I get up from bed and help
      him to scale, clean and salt the fishes.
It is so good: the two of us alone in the kitchen,
once in a while our elbows touch.'
And he says things like:
'I had to fight hard with this one. It glittered like silver, as it
      jumped in the air . . .'
And he makes the gesture with his hand.
The silence of when we first met crosses the kitchen as a deep
      river.
At last the fishes are on the plates and we go sleeping.

[45]

There is a silver glittering in the air:
we are the bride and the groom . . . (*TSC* 31).

'Erotic is the soul', she says in another poem (*B* 66).

Words can do anything. Happiness is thinking, when the body only touches the solid things with its feet, in its rainbow dance of words: we become light, pneumatic entities, winged miracles, floating with the wind . . .

For many years I had a dream: I wanted to plant *my* garden. Not a garden but *my* garden. I say *my* garden because it had to be able to evoke the stories and images I love. Many gardens are delights to the senses but they are dumb. They say nothing. They lack the power to evoke. I walk through their alleys and my inner garden continues to sleep. Yes, there is an inner vegetal world inside our bodies. I remember Rilke's verses:

He loved his inner world,
forests, very old and sleeping,
and their green light
made his heart pulsate . . . (*ED* 17).

I dreamed about planting *my* garden because I couldn't. The plot where my house was built was too small. But one day I managed to buy the vacant plot by the side of my house, and my dream came true.

For those whom I have not told my dreams, my plants are only plants: vegetal entities which offer a bit of pleasure to the body. For me, however, they are magical: they have the power to conjure up the past. The lilac was given by my father. Everytime I smell its odour I see my father's face and hear his voice. The myrtle takes me back to the public garden of my home town. The emperor's jasmin grew in the backyard of my grandfather's huge colonial house, filled with mysteries, where I played as a boy. I walk by my plants. There are invisible presences in their midst. The past becomes present. My garden is a text. Each plant is a poetic metonymy. Many other plants give me pleasure. But my garden gives me joy. Pleasure is an experience which exists only in the present. According to Freud pleasure is discharge of dammed energy, the prototype of which being the orgasm. Once it is achieved the body returns to a state of rest, desireless. It no longer longs for the object. But joy is not discharge. It is reunion. And even when the experience is past, there remains its memory as nostalgia, as when one has just finished hearing one of Mozart's sonatas. One does not wish the end, one wants to prolong it. Nobody cries because of pleasure, but one cries because of joy.

'Please, don't go . . . Please, come back . . .' Plato was right as he said that Eros was the son of Penia and Poros, of poverty and fullness, of loss and possession. In Portuguese we have a word to describe this feeling, and it seems that there is no corresponding word in English: 'saudades': the feeling which one has as one feels the presence of an absence: the toy of the dead child, an old photograph, the letter which has just arrived, the empty room . . . 'Saudades' names this feeling of mutilation: I feel that a part of my own body has been torn out of me. And I say its name, before the void . . .

This word does not describe any given object. Its function is not cognitive. Its function is magical: to evoke. And it returns from where it had been, forgotten . . .

Have you read the love story of Fiorentino Ariza for Firmina Dazza, in Gabriel Garcia Marques' *Love in the Time of Cholera*? It all began when they were very young. She, an adolescent. He, a modest clerk who worked for a navigation company. But in those days daughters did not own their feelings and she was made the wife of a prosperous medical doctor of the town. Poor Fiorentino . . . He almost went out of his mind and his passion was so desperate that he lost his job: his business letters were written as if they were love letters . . . In the town where he lived there was a 'plaza' where incipient lawyers made some extra money writing petitions and legal documents for people. Fiorentino had no inclination to write legal documents, but he was full of love letters, and this is what he advertised and sold. If the costumer was a man, he imagined that the letter was addressed to his beloved Firmina; and when a woman, he imagined the kind of letter he would like to receive from her. One day a young man came to him and told his story. He was desperately in love with a girl, with whom he had never talked before. He wanted Fiorentino to write the first love letter. And so he did. Some days later it was a young woman who looked for him. She had a letter in her hands. The man who had written it had to be beautiful as his words. She was in love, but she did not know what to say. With these words she handed the letter to Fiorentino: it was the letter he had written himself some days before. For some weeks he became involved in a furious love correspondence with himself. And as the letters went through the lovers, they performed what they said and the lovers were transformed in the image and likeness of the words. The story ends by telling that they got married. They discovered what had happened, and when their first child was born Fiorentino was invited to be the godfather . . .

Love words are images inside the mirror: we are the mirror.

The other is beautiful because we see ourselves beautiful in his or her words.

Speaking mirrors, as in Snow White's story. The human-tragic character of the story is not the girl; it is the step-mother and her dialogues with her mirror: someone who once had spoken words which made her beautiful but which then spoke words which made her ugly. The beautiful woman became a witch . . . And she broke the mirror. Black magic: when, by the power of the bewitching word, the beautiful is made ugly.

My father-in-law was born in Germany. He moved to Brazil after the first world war. He was the son of a Seventh-Day Adventist pastor. As you know, members of this religious group are very strict about their eating habits. They do not eat pork and blood, and don't drink liquor, tea or coffee. My father-in-law, even though he was no longer a believer, could not forget the prohibition words which had been written in his body. And he even had an extra prohibition, which was his alone: he could not eat brain. Even though he had never tried brain before, the fact was that he did not like it . . . One day he was invited to a dinner. He was the guest of honour. And he was very pleased as he saw that the main dish was breaded cauliflower. He must have thought that the hostess was an expert in the rules of etiquette: she must have known about his almost vegetarian habits. He ate and had more. Delicious . . . At the end of the dinner, the alchemy of assimilation having already begun, and body and soul satisfied with the food, he gave a compliment.

'The breaded cauliflower was divine . . .'

'Oh! No!' said the hostess. 'It is not breaded cauliflower; it is breaded brain . . .'

Poor lady! She could never have imagined the kind of storm which an innocent word in the mouth could produce in the body . . . My father-in-law, forgetting all rules of propriety, jumped off his chair, rushed to the bath room, and vomited everything . . .

How can we account for what happened?

The 'thing': was it not delicious? Had not the body tasted and approved it? What physical or chemical changes could have occurred after the word 'brain' was said? None. My father-in-law knew this in his head. And yet his body did not agree. What had been good to eat before the word, ceased to be after the word was heard. What strange entity is this, which has the power to bring to nothing the hard realities of physics and chemistry? One single word triggered the digestive storm. It was not the taste, it was not the smell, it was not the touch, it was not the sight: one single word. Which leads us to a strange conclusion: my father-in-law did not vomit a 'thing'; he vomited words. What gives pleasure – and displeasure – are not things, but words, the words which dwell in them. As Zarathustra suggested, what makes things refreshing are the names and sounds which are given to them (*PN* 329). Somehow, for reasons unknown, the word 'cauliflower' was, in my father-in-law's body, the beginning of a beautiful world, whereas the word 'brain' invoked repulsive images. One single word suffices to transform a prince into a frog. No witches are needed. The prince himself can perform the black magic . . .

The body has a philosophy of its own. Reality, for it, is not what we usually call by this name. It is not something given. It is rather the *result* of an alchemic operation whereby a nameless 'stuff' is mixed with words. And its world is created. This, and only this, is what is given to the body to be eaten. Guimarães Rosa showed great familiarity with the wisdom of the body when he said that 'everything is real because everything is invented'. 'Dreams is what we are made of', says Norman O. Brown (*LB* 254). My father-in-law did not vomit the 'thing'. He vomited the bad dreams, nightmares, which were invoked by the bewitching word . . .

My thoughts dance and jump from this disastrous dinner to mediaeval sacramental theology. In describing what took place in the eucharist they used the word transubstantiation. Protestant theologians could not understand this concept because, for them, words have no magical power; they are only raw material for thinking. I suspect that this is due to the fact that their fathers-in-law never experienced the embarrassment of an indigestion provoked by one single word. These two situations: are they not rigorously alike? Bread and wine: the basic 'stuff' for the meal. Then a word is pronounced. Nothing changes. Under the scrutiny of objective criteria of knowledge, bread remains bread and wine remains wine. As mediaeval theologians said, the 'accidents' remain the same. And yet they affirmed that by the power of the word an imperceptible change took place: a new 'substance' is there, in the place of the old: the body and the blood of Christ.

But which word is this, with such a magical power? Is it not the word which announces the absence? Is not the eucharist a meal before the Absent One? 'Eat and drink in remembrance of me' (I Cor. 11.25). If it is done in 'remembrance' it is because something or someone is absent. Bread and wine are physical entities. They serve to nourish the body. Even ants and bees know that. But when certain words are pronounced, a great void is opened inside our bodies, we feel 'saudades', and our bodies are transubstantiated by the power of the absence. The villagers were resurrected because of the power of the Void: they heard words which named their longings. They understood that they are lost, without the help of that which does not exist.

What a strange world – the reality of which is mystically surrounded by a transparent rainbow of absences . . . Its language we no longer know. 'Have you brought the key?', it asks. But we have not. Indeed we have many keys, many words. But we don't know where we have left the key, the word . . .

Our keys open the doors of a world which is familiarly known by all and about which we talk. It is solid, securely tied around hard things, and those who know it have no difficulty in repeating its gospel:

'In the beginning it was the thing . . .'

Words come after, as consequences.

First the original, then the copies.

First the trees, the clouds, the mountains; then their inverted reflections on the surface of the lake.

But we all know that reflections have no reality. They are nothing more than light playing with our eyes. They do not have power. They have meaning, only. They are the finger which points to the moon, but woe to the one who takes the finger for the moon.

But the keys we don't have lead us through the looking glass . . . One dives through the shining surface of the lake, and there the words are no longer reflections but fishes which swim in dark waters: the magical, sacred universe which is hidden inside our flesh. These words are more real than things.

Now it is the things which are the reflections of the word.

In the beginning, before anything existed, and there was nothing to appear reflected on the surface of the waters, there was the Void. No true word could be said because there was nothing to be reflected.

And yet, a word was heard, 'ex nihilo', filling the primordial silence.

It had to be God's word, because it had the power to bring into existence the world which did not exist.

In the beginning, the Word.

[51]

Then, the Universe.
God's mirror. The Word taking on a visible form.
Universe.
uni-Verse.
In hegelian terminology: the objectification of the Spirit.
It is not the Universe which is the meaning of the Word.
It is the Word which is the meaning of the Universe.
It is not the finger which points to the moon.
It is the moon which points to the finger.
The meaning of the universe is
the verse
which lies hidden, unspoken,
inside its silence.
Somehow God is like Narcissus: they both want to see their beauty. But Narcissus was bewitched by the deception of light. And what he loved was only a reflection which could not be embraced. Every time he tried to reach it, his fingers made it disappear, as they touched the water.

God says the Word and the Universe appears, as an object of love: a garden, paradise.

And there, beauty takes on a human form: man and woman, God's image, God's mirror . . .

What is a man? A man is a void: the longing for a woman.

And what is a woman? A woman is a void: the longing for a man.

They are what they lack . . .

Speech is masculine: it goes out and penetrates, in order to give pleasure and impregnate. The seed longs for the earth . . . Through the word I put my semen inside another person.

Hearing is feminine. The ear is a void, waiting for the word which will bring pleasure and life.

But the anatomical separation of the sexes is more than a biological accident. Man and woman, without separation and without confusion, as in the christological dogma, God's image. Eternal loss, eternal longing. God is both masculine and feminine, father and mother, man and woman, desire for the other.

[52]

This was Narcissus' tragedy: he did not long for what he did not have; there was no void in his body; he could not dream. Our secret is androgyny . . . Happiness is not pleasure; it is reunion with the gracious mirror which lets the image which abides in our void to be seen.

The dead man did not deliver any pleasure. He couldn't. He was dead. But in his void the lost images returned. He became the mirror where the dreams of the villagers returned.

Psychoanalysis also reads the same gospel. Indeed, it is nothing but a long commentary about the same sacred text.

> In the beginning was the Word,
> and the Word became flesh . . .

Mythical time . . .
As happens with fairy tales, it cannot be understood literally. The 'once upon a time in a far distant land' is a metaphorical way of speaking about what is being told in and by the body, now. The body has no past and no future. Memories are the way the body has of talking about its void. And hopes are its way of expressing its longing for reunion. 'I sing, yes, I sing the present, and also the past and the future', says Alvaro de Campos. 'Because the present is the whole past, the whole future' (*PAC* 145). Cosmic spaces are the inner face of the body. As Cecília Meireles put it in a poem about her grandmother,

> Your body was a thinking mirror of the universe (*FP* 144).

The whole universe dwells inside our bodies. Feuerbach's theology is built upon this foundation. He says: 'In the object which man contemplates he becomes acquainted with himself. We know the man by the object, by his conception of what is external to himself. Even the objects which are the most remote from man, *because* they are objects to him, are revelations of the human nature. Even the moon, the sun, the stars, call man "Gnothi seauton"' (*EC* 5). In Ricoeur's words, 'everything which is symbolized is the body'. 'The only scripture is the human body itself; what happens to the person's own body . . . is

[53]

identical with what happens to the universe' (*LB* 224, 226). The mythical poems about the origins of the world are dreams about the origin of the body.

'In the beginning of our bodies is the word'.

'Speech does not abide in man', says Martin Buber; 'but man takes his stand in speech . . .' (*IT* 39).

The mythical story of creation begins with the universe and ends with the body. But as it often happens with dreams, the order must be reversed. It is not the universe which contains the body; it is the body which contains the universe . . . The world dwells in the body; the universe is the visible face of the body's deepest dream: paradise . . .

Two opposed themes: Western thought has played a set of 'variations' on them . . .

Where do we belong?

Where is home?

Some say that we belong to the surface of the lake, where reflections are clear and distinct. There is where we should build our houses.

But some play the reverse theme. We belong to the darkness of the waters, where the eyes are unable to see. The body is a mysterious lake. Inside its deep waters, our name lies, asleep . . .

It is well known that Luther said that reason was a whore. Few, however, know, that this was his reply to Erasmus' statement that the body is a whore . . .

Erasmus was a citizen of the world of light. Luther, however, knew that amidst the glitter of reflections, Lucifer, the deceiver, is the one who bears the light (from the Latin 'lux', light, and 'ferre', to bear). Truth abides in the darkness of the body where a word is heard. Not the eyes, but the ears. Truth is 'a Poem which became Flesh', the body of Christ, ubiquitous and hidden in the whole universe, even in the tiniest leaf of a tree.

The villagers could not do anything; they were also dead. Something had to be done to them: it was not their doing. In the utter impotence and silence of death, the forgotten words began to be heard. And they awoke from their slumber.

The villagers dreamed. And their bodies were possessed by their dreams. They began telling stories and they even thought that they were talking about the dead man. But in dreams the body only speaks about its void. The words spoke themselves, out of the deep waters where they were sleeping. This is what in psychoanalytical language has the name of 'unconscious'. 'The unconscious is nothing more than language, as it is alive and as it is spoken against the conscious intentions of the subject . . .' (*JL* 68).

It is not our doing. It is the doing of an 'Unknown' . . .

In theological language: not justification by works but justification by grace. Grace is the forgotten word which speaks itself . . . We are all feminine. We are the Virgin who is made pregnant by the Word which comes with the Wind.

A word is heard and the body trembles. But this trembling is only possible if body and word are the same thing. 'Words are the stuff with which we are made', says Octávio Paz (*AL* 37).

Our bodies dwell in oblivion, like the Sleeping Beauty. We no longer know how to play the tune which is written in our flesh. The reflections, ten thousand, we know. But the depth of the lake is beyond our reason. We learned that we are where we think: 'I think, therefore I am.' Now, the reversed theme: 'Where I think, there I am not.'

This is what poets have been saying all the time. No wonder that they have become marginal. They should not be invited to our academic dinner parties, because they speak as if they were drunk.

'What is the use of deciphering pictograms of ten thousand years ago', asks Carlos Drummond de Andrade, 'if I don't even know how to decypher the writing which is inside me? I question dubious signs and their kaleidoscopic variations, observing them second by second. The essential truth is the unknown which dwells in me . . .' (*C* 29).

Our beauty sleeps, forgotten, as in the story.

Fernando Pessoa has a marvellous poem in which he describes the sleeping princess, in the tower of the castle, vegetal life all around her, ivy leaves already covering her face like a veil. The prince, coming from afar, not knowing the way, moving ahead in ignorance, through dark and misty trails. Till he arrives

> where in sleep she dwells.
> And still faint from the ride
> his hand gropes for her face
> and pulls the ivy veil aside.
> And, to his surprise he sees
> that the sleeping princess
> no other person than he himself, is . . . (*PFP* 239).

We dwell in oblivion.
We don't know how to pray.
We have forgotten the name of our deepest desire.
Our sighs are too deep for words.
Our body speaks in tongues . . .

In former times, when writing was done on leather, it was common to erase a text in order to write a new one. The words were scraped off and the rough surface was made smooth again with the help of ivory. When the eyes were assured that nothing of the old text was left, new writing was done. And the old one was gone for ever . . . But they did not know that deep inside the leather the old text remained, invisible. Today, thanks to modern techniques, it can be recovered again. These were the palimpsests: leather on which many texts were written.

Our bodies are palimpsests.

There is a superficial text, visible to all: the surface of the lagoon.

But in the darkness of the waters another story is being silently told. Once in a while it emerges, wearing masks, speaking in tongues.

Fractures in the flesh, physical symptoms. Groddeck, one of the discoverers of psychoanalysis, realized that diseases are strangled messages. They are not accidents which happen to the body. They are ideograms which the body itself writes, in a desperate effort to be heard and understood.

Sometimes as dreams, cryptic images which make themselves visible when the lights are turned off and the Ego – the lord of the lights – is off to sleep.

Sometimes the fishes jump out of the water even in day time, they are seen for a split-second, but soon disappear again inside the lagoon . . .

If, by any chance, the body remembers the forgotten Word which abides in its flesh as a love story, it finds its way back home. It is possessed by its dreams and is resurrected from death because, as Blake once said, 'the Eternal Body of Man is The Imagination' (*PB* 497). We are resurrected by the power of that which does not exist.

Life comes from the dead man of the sea:

baptism, diving into the depths of the dark waters . . .

And then, one is a child again . . .

And the village is never the same again . . .

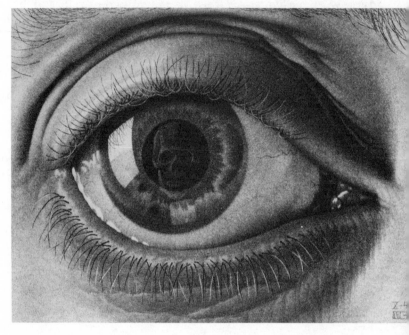

Chapter IV

WHAT REALLY HAPPENED

If you describe the world just as it is there will be
in your words nothing but many lies and no truth.
                                                                    Tolstoi

Knowledge is a polite word for dead but not
                    buried imagination.
                                                            e e cummings

Gabriel Garcia Marques' report, as we remember it, ends with the laconic statement that 'the village was never the same again'. But no hints are given as to what really took place after the visit of the dead man. It seems that the villagers themselves did not have any interest in documenting their experiences in the AD time (after the dead man), because fishermen lack the sense of the importance of historical records. They were happy with simply living. There are indications, however, that the story became a sort of oral tradition which circulated widely from mouth to mouth throughout the whole country reaching even foreign lands. Obviously it provoked reactions which ranged from incredulity to amazement. The village became a centre of touristic interest and many curious travellers included it in their itineraries. The reports of their visits are practically the only source of information we have. These reports do not have the rigour demanded by historical objectivity and must be taken with a grain of salt. But since this is all that is extant, we have no alternatives left but to start off from what they said. We find ourselves in a position similar to that of a person who has to put together the pieces of a jig-saw-puzzle, having only a few fragments of the whole. The empty spaces must be filled with constructions of the imagination.

All reports are unanimous in describing an event which seems to have become the centre of the village life. The villagers, after sunset, would gather daily on the beach, around a fire, and they told stories about that portentous day. What was most remarkable, it is said, was not *what* they said but rather *how* they said it. Some witnesses say that it was as if they were drunk. Could it be that the story had an effect similar to that of hallucinogenic drugs? It might be. The fact was that the act of retelling the story provoked perceptible changes in their bodies, giving the impression that they were 'possessed' by spirits – or by the Spirit. They did not speak about the dead man only. It was a sort of 'linguistic game', similar to the one described by Herman Hesse in his book *The Glass Bead Game*. Someone would say an initial word, which functioned as the 'theme', to be followed by endless variations, in a fashion which resembles the music style named 'variations on a given theme'. Others compared it to the Japanese chain of poems called 'renku', which is composed along similar lines. Images floated freely around the central theme, in a dance of free associations. Their talk constructed an enchanted world and, if it is true, as a known philosopher said, that 'the limits of language denote the limits of the world', it is fair to conclude that theirs was, in fact, an enchanted world. Some witnesses even say that it was in one of these gatherings that João Guimarães Rosa suddenly realized that 'everything is real because everything is invented'. From memories of the past they jumped to hopes about the future: remembrance became prophecy. And they composed poems about deserts being transformed into gardens, lions eating straw with cows, children playing with snakes, weapons being beaten into plowshares, and adults becoming light and playful like children. True, this was poetry. But the villagers took it with utter seriousness, as if it were true. There are some phantastic stories about people walking on water, crossing over abysses on rainbow bridges and even flying.

It is reported, also, that some amazing changes were to be observed in their practical life. Their economic habits, for instance, experienced a reversal. During the BD time (before the dead man) their attitudes towards money could be described as dominated by the 'saving' motif. And for good reasons. Since they could not see any perspectives of change in the village, what they hoped for in the future was to move somewhere else. And this demanded money. So, they worked hard, lived very ascetic lives, spent only what was strictly necessary for survival, and saved what was left. This combination of hard work and asceticism created a peculiar ethos which even became the object of a careful scientific study by Max Weber, a well known scientist who had been there in BD times. Another philosopher who had visited the village even before, Karl Marx, came to similar conclusions, and noted that this ethos had the result of deforming the sensual life of people. The body ceased to be an *end*, it became a *means* for saving, and all the senses, which are the organs of pleasure, were repressed to the point of being supressed (*PE*; *MCM* 132, 144). But after the great event, instead of saving, they began to spend. This new attitude towards life was celebrated at regular intervals in lavish feasts named potlatch, which were marked by great profusion of food and gifts, often accompanied by destruction of property of the hosts.

Such curious feasts, which are totally incomprehensible from the angle of a saving inspired psychology, were a sure indication that the villagers had undergone a radical reorientation in their feeling of time. In saving, the present is emptied, it becomes only a *means* for something in the future; life is postponed. Spending, on the contrary, is possible only if one is not anxious about the future and is committed to life in the present. Poets made use of metaphors to describe this change, and said that it was as if water-holding cisterns had been transformed in overflowing springs.

The appearance of their houses changed, also. In the BD times there was no concern for the building of new houses, and the old ones were barely preserved, often reaching a ruined condition. Only essential repairs were made, when walls were cracked and in danger of falling down, and rain went through the tiles. Repainting was never done and their colours had reached a uniform dust colour. This can be easily explained. It is unwise to spend money in old and new houses if one is about to leave the place. Their gardens, in their turn, were planted according to strictly utilitarian criteria: only things to eat were to be found in them. Flowers were not cultivated, and the only ones which were left were those which grew wild in the fields. Instead of trees, which take too long to grow, they preferred planting pumpkins. This situation was totally reversed in the AD times. It seems that the villagers began to feel that that was a good place to live and that it was worth 'planting in it the seed of their highest hope'. It is even reported that a man (later to be recognized as a prophet) who had been saving money for his escape, took all his silver coins and bought a piece of land, sealing the transaction with the words: 'Houses and fields and vineyards shall again be bought in this land.' This same man, on another occasion, ordered the villagers to take wives and bear children, to multiply and not to decrease, because to them 'a future and a hope' had been given (Jer. 29.11;32). Indeed, many new houses were built, the old ones were repaired, and all were painted with lively colours, even the poorest. Pregnant women and babies began to be seen moving around, a sure indication that there had been a revival of the pleasures of love-making. The visitors also report that adults had a great interest in play, which is an activity totally void of economic interest, since it produces nothing, except pleasure. Adults often appeared mixed with children in their games and it seems that they did not feel a bit embarrassed. Prominent among their leisure activities was kite-flying and when they were asked about this preference they replied that this was the activity with which they were most identified. It seems that they saw the kites as metaphors of themselves. Some maintain that it was during one of these visits that a writer, to become famous later, got the inspiration for the title of his book 'the unbearable lightness of being'.

All reports, irrespective of their differences, agreed on two points. First, it could not be denied that 'something' had happened which changed the village. And second: this 'something' had to do with the dreaming experiences related to the story-telling games.

But there is another tradition according to which the story had a different end. Gabriel Garcia Marques must have ignored it, because he makes no reference to this alternate version of the facts. Those who have studied the matter are unanimous in identifying his version as belonging to the earliest oral tradition and there is even the possibility that he was an eye-witness. The second version must have appeared much later — and this accounts for Marques' silence.

The extant documents of this tradition (which, for reasons to be explained later, came to be known as 'Source E') were produced by a group of people who separated themselves from the village and became organized as a monastic esoteric order. A number of hypotheses have been proposed in order to explain this obscure event. It is certain that the miracle was not effective for all. Some remained untouched by the magic of the dead man and consequently did not have the transforming experience. They remained outside of the circle of the 'new reality'. There was a break in communication. To the extent that language determines the limits of the world, they began to live in different universes. The two groups could no longer get engaged in meaningful conversation and they became strangers to one another because 'the subjective reality of the world hangs on the thin thread of conversation', as Peter Berger remarks (*SC* 17). Two incommensurable universes began to exist, side by side. Thus, even before the monastic order existed as an institution, it already existed as a linguistic fact. Language unites and separates. What was sense, for a group, was non-sense to the other. Wisdom is folly, folly is wisdom; beauty is ugliness, ugliness is beauty. (This curious phenomenon has been suggested poetically by a number of thinkers, among them Nietzsche, Uexküll and Feuerbach.) For a caterpillar nothing is more beautiful than caterpillar things. In their world even gods are caterpillars. Butterflies, obviously, will retort: 'Non-sense . . .' (*PN* 42, *SB* 159, *EC* 8).

The behaviour of those who had undergone the experience began to be a cause of embarrassment and even ridicule to those who remained outside the enchanted circle. Youngsters, for instance, could not hide their shame when they perceived that their parents had rediscovered the joys of sex. In their own separate reality, sex and old age could not be mixed. And the shame became unbearable when their mothers began to show signs of pregnancy. There is even the legend about a very old couple: she became pregnant against all hope, and this event provoked an outburst of laughter, which was started by the woman herself. It is obvious that this laughter had different meanings. For the outsiders it meant ridicule, but for the villagers it was an explosion of joy. And they even decided to preserve the memory of this event in the name of the boy. He was baptized Isaac, which means laughter. And his mother Sarah, interpreted this choice of a name with the words: 'God has given me good reason to laugh, and everybody who hears will laugh with me' (Gen. 21.6).

To the members of the order, however, this laughter was not a sign of joy but rather an evidence of madness. The villagers, so they argued, had become blind to reality, had regressed to an infantile phase of their psychic development and their behaviour was a sort of collective psychosis: they took their dreams as if they were real. And since they did not want to be infected by this disease, they decided to move away from the village. And this was how the order came into existence and monasteries were built. They all agreed that their symbol should be a lamp, as an expression of their commitment to light and of their horror of darkness and dreaming. They called themselves the 'Enlightened' and saw their mission as educating mankind for reality. This is why their extant documents came to be known as 'Source E'.

The 'Enlightened' affirmed that life cannot be built on dreams. Dreams are disturbances of our mental processes which grow out of the original sin which abides in our body. The body, one of their philosophers said, operates according to the demands of the 'pleasure principle' – and this is how dreams are born. But reality is insensitive to our dreams. The body, the members of the sect did not tire of repeating, is a whore. It has no love for truth. It believes that it has the power to call into existence things that do not exist. And out of this madness it proceeds to make love with the figments of its imagination. Is not poetry an expression of such a madness? The poet makes love with words, ignoring that words have no reality. They are nothing more than reflections inside a mirror. Poetry is, indeed, as play and dreaming, a delightful folly. But nothing more than that. Poetry gives no knowledge. It does not say how things are. It is not a faithful mirror. It cannot, therefore, be the foundation of anything. The images with which poets play are only expressions of the movements 'inside' our bodies, which have nothing to do with the world outside. And the members of the order baptized these emotional images as 'secondary qualities', in order to make clear that they cannot be taken as the foundation for the construction of the world.

If the body and its productions cannot be the 'beginning', it cannot be the 'end' either. The body must be overcome. As opposed to the 'whore', the 'immaculate conception' of all things. So, the members of the order did not speak about the 'resurrection of the body', as the villagers did. They spoke about the 'immortality of the soul', instead.

The body, because it is heavy and has no wings (something that the villagers seemed to ignore) drowns easily in water, and it should beware of jumping lightly over unsteady stones. It should not move until it is sure that the stone is firmly grounded, beyond any possible doubt. In case of doubt it is better to remain still. 'I shall proceed by setting aside all that in which the least possible doubt could be supposed to exist, just as if I had discovered that it was absolutely false', said the most famous of philosophers of the order. 'Archimedes', he proceeds, 'in order that he might draw the terrestrial globe out of its place, and transport it elsewhere, demanded only that one point should be fixed and immovable; in the same way I shall have the right to conceive any hopes if I am happy enough to discover one thing only which is certain and indubitable' (*M* 77).

This way of thinking had visible effects in their ways of walking. Just by watching how a person walked it was possible to identify the group to which it belonged. The villagers went around hopping and dancing, as children do, which was an expression of how they felt inside: light creatures, with winged bodies. The Enlightened, on the contrary, were solemn and grave and marched with steady steps, slowly, testing the ground to see if it was a firm foundation. This difference was also visible in the ways they spoke. The villagers made use of poetry and by the use of metaphors they jumped over immense abysses of time and space: from apples to childhood memories, from a wheat field to a golden hair, from fish-cleaning to deep rivers of love, from bread and wine to the body and the blood of a beloved person, absent. The members of the sect, on the contrary, moved from one word to another only after they had succeeded in building solid bridges of evidences and proof. 'We must proceed carefully', they never tired of saying. It was then that someone realized the close relationship which there exists between ways of walking and ways of speaking. Poetry is dancing; prose is marching. It is obvious that the members of the order were very much afraid of the embarrassment of stumbling, a risk which one has to run if one wants to dance.

The Enlightened wanted to find the firm foundation. Two lines of research were developed. One of them, of historical inspiration, wanted to establish the real facts of the life of the dead man. The other, of hermeneutical inspiration, looked for his 'ipsissima verba' – his very words, and the meanings that were in his mind, when he uttered them.

The first line of investigation produced an overwhelming mass of historical studies which, together, came to be known as 'the quest for the historical dead man'. It is widely recognized that this was the 'greatest achievement' of the order.

Their point of departure was historical. The dead man must have lived in a definite place and in a definite time. It had to be possible, therefore, with the help of historical-critical methods, to reconstruct his life and character. What they wanted – and they liked to say it in German – was to know 'wie es eigentlich gewesen ist' – how it really happened. They wanted to know the historical truth about the dead man, in order both to save him from the web of dreams in which he had been entangled by the villagers' stories, and to save the villagers from their own foolishness.

The research was done on the tacit presupposition that the past is the foundation of the present and that the present is intelligible only as a consequence of the past.

This scientific position, as it can be easily seen, is at loggerheads with the unspoken theory of the villagers. For them the beginning of time was not the past, but the present. The apple that I eat is not to be explained by its seed. It is a reality in itself. I don't need to know the seed in order to enjoy the apple. The flower is not the manure in which it grew. To know the dead man, they said, it is to know the benefit that he does to me, in the present. Every lover who wants to know the past of the beloved person first, in order to be sure of his or her love, is not indeed loving. The villagers had, thus, a curious way of understanding time. As against the familiarly known chronological order of events, in which past comes before the present, they believed that the past comes into existence as a sort of reverberation of the present. The past which abides in my body is a 'variation' on a theme which is alive in the present. The past is the present experienced as longing. Their stories, so they explained, were a transfiguration of resurrection of a dead past, by the power of their present experience of dreaming. 'But it is not real', said the members of the order. 'Its reality is attested by its being alive in the present', the villagers replied. The proof of the pudding is to eat it . . .

Obviously this cannot be true of historical time. The members of the order, as a consequence, and in harmony with their philosophy, decreed that there should not be any more any story-telling to their children, since stories dwell in the world of dreams. Stories were displaced by history.

As time passed by many scholars became so absorbed in their studies that the past, itself, became the end of their lives. And a curious 'variation' of their processional style of walking began to be observed, to the amazement of all: some started walking backwards. One of the villagers, with an ironical smile, remarked mockingly that 'by searching out origins one becomes a crab. The historian looks backward: eventually he also believes backward' (*PN* 470).

Their investigations determined where the dead man had lived, the village where he was born, at the other side of the sea. Many documents were found there which helped them in their historical reconstruction.

But here the researchers were divided. Some rested satisfied with the testimonies found in the extant documents and were of the opinion that their reports were true. They affirmed that these documents were dependable narratives of 'wie es eigentlich gewesen ist'. They came to be identified by their constant repetition of the slogan 'it is written'. 'It is written': this fact brought their search to its end. They had found the foundation they were looking for. The other group was more sceptical. They had developed the 'art of mistrust' and were suspicious that the same thing which had happened in their village could have happened also in the village where the dead man had lived. They suspected that much of what was written was also a product of dreaming. If this were the case, even those 'scriptures' were not dependable; they could not be the foundation they were looking for. So, they decided to dig deeper, in order to find, mixed with those fragments of myths, poetry and gossip, what had actually taken place. They were of the same opinion as Paul Veyne who sees historical records as a products of 'intrigue', since they are inevitably tinged with the desires and dreams of those who wrote them (*CEH* 44). The 'scriptures' could not be accepted as faithful mirrors. But their historical-critical methods, so they claimed, had ways of by-passing the net-work of intrigues in order to arrive at the historical truth. The researchers, who called themselves 'scientific', mocked openly of their colleagues, on account of their naiveté: they did not realize that they had simply exchanged the stories of one village for the stories of another. But the fact is that, irrespective of their methodological differences, they were all moved by the same quest: they were after the historical foundations. They were fundamentalists.

But, as we mentioned before, there was another line of investigation in the quest of the historical dead man. What they had was a corpse, and they knew that it was full of words. But they were written in a language nobody understood, the language of silence.

The villagers told stories about him and for them that sufficed. If their stories transformed them into winged creatures, what other proofs should be required? We have already mentioned their epistemological principle: 'to know the dead man is to know his benefits'. The 'wie es eigentlich gewesen ist' was for them meaningless before their present experience. The ultimate criterion of truth is not a historical event, lost in the past, but the resurrection of the dead, in the present.

The 'Enlightened', however, replied that those stories were nothing but dreams. They could not be true. And they asked about the true meanings which were written in that dead body.

'What were his "ipsissima verba" – his very words?'

'When he spoke, what did he want to say?'

Words are not enough. They are slippery fishes, misty creatures which invoke many different meanings at the same time. One faces the words as one faces the dead man: they are a riddle to be decyphered, a darkness to be dispelled . . .

Interpretation is to bring light where there was darkness,

to exchange equivocal for univocal meanings,

to transform poetry into prose.

Words couldn't be the sure foundation they were looking for. Beyond the Babel of words, the scientific understanding which comes with 'clear and distinct ideas'. Not the word which is a creature of the body, but ideas which are creatures of pure mind.

And, traps and cages in their hands, they moved to the past, through the labyrinth of words, in order to catch their true meanings.

They worked for many years. Science demands patience. Finally they were ready to return to the village in order to tell the truth.

It was told that it was after sunset when they arrived.

The first stars were already visible on the skies, and the full moon was over the horizon. The villagers were gathered on the beach, as they used to, their faces dimly illuminated by the fire around which they sat. They told stories and the universe was filled with the absence of the dead man. Children silently heard their parents speaking:

'Once upon a time, when this village was dead, the sea brought us a gift, the body of a dead man . . .'

But suddenly the stories were interrupted by the noise and voices of approaching people. They had lamps in their right hands and caged birds on their left . . .

'We found the truth, we know the truth about the dead man', they shouted triumphantly.

'Please, tell us your stories', the villagers said to the newcomers.

The villagers were all silent and smiled as the Enlightened began telling the truth. But they did not tell stories. They opened thick books, treatises, commentaries, confessions – the crystallized results of their work. And it is reported that, as they spoke, the stars began to fade away till they disappeared, and dark clouds covered the moon. The sea was suddenly silent and the warm breeze became a cold wind.

When they finished telling the truth of history and interpretation the villagers returned to their homes. And, no matter how hard they tried, they could not remember the stories they used to tell. And they slept dreamless sleep.

As to the members of the order, after so many years of hard scientific work, they had their first night of sound sleep, also without dreams. Their mission was accomplished. They had, finally, told the truth.

And it is reported that the village returned to be what it had been, before it had been resurrected by the gift of the sea . . .

Chapter V

WORDS WHICH ARE GOOD TO BE EATEN

The tempter approached him and said, 'If you are the Son of God, tell those stones to become bread.' Jesus answered, 'Scripture says, "Man cannot live by bread alone; he lives on every word that proceeds out of the mouth of God."'

(Matt. 4.2)

I went to the angel and asked him to give me the little scroll. He said to me, 'Take it and eat it.'

(Rev. 10.10)

Words which resurrect the dead . . .

The two stories about the village are variations about this *leitmotif*. A special kind of words, words which have power to penetrate the flesh, to make love with it and make it pregnant with life. Words which are of the same substance as the body. Otherwise, how could they become one flesh?

This is the only theological theme. Theology is an exercise about the marriage of Word and flesh, an endless poem about the mystery of the incarnation. Words and flesh make love and the body is born . . .

Word and flesh,
without separation,
without confusion,
and yet
one single body.

The biblical story says that it happened 'once upon a time, in a far distant land'. But, as we already know, stories have power only because their past and distance are metaphors for the here and now. They never actually happened, so that they can happen always, everywhere. Snow White's step mother is me, the Sleeping Beauty is me, Oedipus is me, Narcissus is me. Stories are not windows; they are mirrors. The story of the incarnation is my own story, my forgotten past and my hidden future. Christology is anthropology. Christology is biography. The mystery of God is the mystery of our own bodies.

But we have misunderstood it, and we ask, like the little girl: 'Did it really happen?' We look in the mirror and we mistake it for a window. And thus we don't know the place where Word and flesh make love . . .

Some believed that they make love under the full light of midday sun. And they look for luminous words, in which there is no darkness. 'If we are able to know, if we succeed in producing a science of this portentous event, then we will be resurrected', they say. They think that the eyes are the gates of the body, and that the body is made pregnant through the eyes. Their supreme goal is 'the beatific *vision* of God'. And they turn the lights on because, without light, the eyes don't see.

But all lovers know that too much light is not good for love. Love demands a bit of darkness. Maybe because light is a creature which only moves on the surface of things. One sees when light, having hit the surface of something, bounces back, in a reflection. Light is impotent to penetrate. But love demands depth, penetration, something that light is incapable of doing. The body, indeed, shuns from too much light. It fears full visibility. When man and woman saw that they were naked, they hid their bodies from the eyes behind the fig leaves. The flesh does not make love with light . . .

Maybe because the body's original Word was born in a place where there is no light. It was born in the mouth. Indeed, this Word was already in the mouth long before the mouth was able to say any word.

Mouth is the place of eating long before it is the place of speaking. Eating preceeds speaking. Our original Word is a twin sister of food. When Ludwig Feuerbach, a professional of words, said that 'we are what we eat' (man ist was man isst) he pointed to the place where Word and flesh make love. 'I eat, therefore I am'. Eating comes before speaking. And speaking, throughout our whole lives, is a form of eating.

We are what we eat . . . The new born baby, even though it is an 'infans' – which in Latin means a dumb body, still before the birth of speech – already knows what the philosopher meant. The child knows the wisdom of eating. It is in the hungry mouth that the first wordless 'lesson' about life is given, a lesson which is prior to any word and which is the beginning of all words. All words to be written in the future are variations around the theme of hunger, regardless of their apparent oblivion of this inaugural moment. We speak because our being is hungry. I believe that Fernando Pessoa, who once said that 'to think is to be sick in the eyes' would agree with me if I say that 'to speak is to be sick in the body, to be hungry'. Words are substitutes for the food we don't have. Mallarmé, who had the dream of writing a book with one single word, would envy this child who silently sucks the mother's breast. It dwells in a wordless poem. An interpreter of dreams could have told him that what he desired was to return to the condition of a child, in order to witness the birth of the first word.

The mouth of the 'infans' already knows the fundamental metaphysics: reality is not made up of 'thought' and 'matter' as we have been taught. Reality is made up of 'hunger' and of an 'obscure object of desire', which will satisfy it. Even before having ever touched the mother's breast, the mouth sucks the void, confident that it exist.

Hunger and food,
void and fulness,
desire and satisfaction . . .
And Augustine would add: the restless heart and God . . .

The sucking mouth knows that life is not its possession. It must come from outside. It is a gift. It is grace. Its rhythmic movements, sucking the void – the first poem – are a prayer, the original prayer: 'The breast comes . . .'

The mouth learns, then, the second lesson: life and pleasure are joined in the same object. The breast is not only a milk-delivering device. It is not only a means to life. It is an end in itself, an object of fruition. As the child sucks the breast, it enjoys blessedness . . .

Eating is living;
Eating is pleasure.

This is our original dream, the original utopia, the original program of the 'pleasure principle'; the unity between life and pleasure. All other dreams, both individual and social, are variations around it.

The mouth learns then the third lesson: the world outside is divided between things which are good to be eaten, and things which are not good to be eaten: food and non-food, things to be taken inside the body and things to remain outside the body. Good and evil, the primordial ethics of the body.

We are what we eat. Alexander Schmemann, the Russian-orthodox theologian, comments:

> Long before Feuerbach the same definition of man was given by the Bible. In the biblical story of creation man is presented as a hungry being and whole world as his food. Man must eat in order to live; he must take the whole world into his body and transform it into himself, into flesh and blood. He is, indeed, what he eats, and the whole world is presented as one all-embracing banquet table for man. And this image of the banquet remains, throughout the whole Bible, the central image of life. It is the image of life at its creation and also at its end and fulfilment: 'that you eat and drink at my table in my kingdom' (*FLW* 1).

The first Word appears as an expression of longing, when paradise is lost. It is a 'rainbow bridge' that our heart builds over things eternally apart . . . It names the void. When the child, after having experienced the original blessedness, is hungry again, and the breast is absent, it fantasizes the absent breast. The body puts an image in the place of food: privation becomes bearable because of this word, a word to be eaten.

Jesus tells the Tester that he was able to bear the suffering of hunger because there were eating words in his provisions. And the angel, in the book of Revelation, tells the seer not to read, not to understand but to eat the little scroll. Words and food are made out of the same stuff. They are both born of the same mother, hunger. And if it is true that 'in the beginning it was the Word', it must be added that the Word was uttered because of hunger. God is hunger, God is love: it is the same thing. These are metaphorical ways of pointing to the same longed for object, which must become one with the body.

The original Word was born in darkness. The child's eyes were closed. Proximity abolishes the eyes. If the object is too close, its contours get blurred. To kiss with open eyes is not to kiss. The eyes are not needed in this moment of happiness. The original symbol abides in darkness. There is 'delight' when the child sucks the breast, but there is 'no light' . . .

Eye-symbols dwell in distance and separation.

Mouth-symbols express reunion and possession.

It is not by accident that in many languages the supreme experience of enjoyment of two bodies, the sexual act, is named as 'eating'.

But paradise was lost. We are no longer the child . . . And we learn another lesson: the world outside is no breast. It is useless to cry. No mother will come . . . Our mouth is open, it is hungry. But the world is not good to eat. It is hard, raw, bitter, sour . . . But, as it happened with the child, the body has not forgotten. 'What memory loves is eternal', says Adélia Prado. The original Word remains hidden, and yet alive in the depths of our flesh. As Freud once put it, our original program was established by the 'pleasure principle'. And we fantasy the return of our first eating experience, when hunger and breast were mystically united. If reality is hard, raw, bitter and sour, something must be done, so that it will be transformed into food. It is not enough to describe things as they are. They must be changed. Marx stated the problem and pointed to its solution: 'the philosophers have only interpreted the word in various ways; the point, however, is to change it.'

The child's experience was magical. A cry was enough to conjure up the breast. Now the breast has been taken away from us, and no cry will perform the miracle.

But we have found a way out of this dualism in which desire and its obscure object are eternally apart. We have mixed the fire of desire with reality, and thus cooking was invented. Cooking is an alchemic operation whereby the raw, by the magic of fire, is transformed in food . . .

The members of the monastic order did not know anything about cooking. They believed that the body is moved by the eyes. And so they affirmed that 'we see, therefore we are'. They were scientists and professors and their being lived in the classroom. The villagers, on the contrary, knew that 'we are what we eat', and their being found its home in the kitchen. They were cooks . . .

So, even at the risk of breaking the rules of etiquette, I invite you to pass from the classroom to the kitchen, from words which are good to be thought to words which are good to be eaten . . .

Kitchen is a place of transformations. Nothing is allowed to remain the same. Fire and its allies are at work . . . Things come in raw, as nature produced them. And they go out different, according to the demands of pleasure. The hard must be softened. Smells and tastes which were dormant inside are forced to come out: cooking is to give the magic kiss which wakes up sleeping pleasures. Alchemy, metamorphoses: cooking joins what nature has separated. Space is abolished. Salt, garlic, pepper, sugar, thyme, clove, parsley, oregano, cinnamon, paprika, cumin, celery, sage, tarragon, horseradish, curry powder, they are all invited, from the distant lands where they grow, to join the festival of cooking. The sweet, the sour, the bitter and the salty are forced to enter into non-existant combinations. Everything is a new creature, everything is made anew.

Leaven, this silent ally of fire, does its work without noise. Beverages of all kinds, unknown to nature: wine, beer, brandy, bourbon, whisky, vodka, sake, each in its own way, are liquids in which 'spirits' lie bottled. New tastes and smells appear. And also new colours and shapes. Cooking is also a plastic art. What is good to be eaten must also be good to be seen. The eyes gain a new potency. Linked to the mouth and to the nose, they are given the power to taste. Reds, greens, yellows, browns, whites are set in kaleidoscopic combinations. And water, milk and oil celebrate alliances with the fire. Even those things which seem to be served raw are never served as they were taken from nature. Tomatoes, lettuce, radishes, watercress, cabbage, they all come transformed by the taste, smell and touch of dressings. And the pans, frying pans, knives, forks, spoons, ovens and stoves are all mediators in this feast, the end of which is the pleasure of the body. The kitchen knows augustinian theology: in it the order of 'uti' never forgets that it exists only for the sake of the 'frui': the purpose of work is joy: the six days of creation find their fulfilment when paradise is offered as a gift to the delight of both God and man.

But the kitchen, alone, is dead. For it to live, a soul is needed: the cook. The cook knows that we are hungry beings. He knows that we are what we eat. Animals also know that. But they do not cook. Their desire is tame: they eat the raw. They are beings of nature. The cook knows that our hunger is infinite. Nature does not satisfy it. Our hunger is not a thing of the body. It comes out of our soul. The Tester suggests that Jesus should solve his biological problem. He should be practical. After forty days of fasting, the body needs food. But Jesus replies that his hunger, no bread could ever satisfy it. He longed for an absent food, the only evidence for it being the Word.

The cook also lives from words. He eats words even before he does his work. Fire is always burning and pots are always boiling in his imagination. His eyes see invisible colours, his nose feels absent smells, his mouth tastes non-existing tastes. And his body is possessed by the meal which has not been prepared, yet. His imagination is a kitchen and a banquet. He lives in the future. He is an eschatological being. If we were to write a treatise with the title *Critique of the Cooking Reason* it is sure that its first chapter would be dedicated to hunger. But hunger alone would not be enough, unless the cook were able to name the things we long for.

And he says these names. Recipes. He names what he wants to eat. He names what he believes the others would like to eat. Pleasurable food. And, by the power of these words, he calls, joins, mixes, adds, subtracts, roasts, boils, bakes, fries. Before his food is served at the table it is eaten in his dreams . . . And, by dreaming, he 'brings to life in his body that which does not exist' (*RR* xi).

The objects we long for are not ready, in nature. Cooking is the art of making real what is unreal, of making present what is absent: a eucharistic metaphor.

The kitchen is a definite space; we know where it is located. But its soul is not there. It lies in the dreams of the cook. The kitchen is a utopian space. Yes, he must know . . . He must know the powers of the fire, the properties of the water, the secret of the alchemic transformations, the rhythm of time. If he did not know reality, how could he ever cook? His food would be nothing but dreams inside his head. And they would not have power to deliver pleasure to body. Knowledge of reality is part of cooking reason. But this knowledge is not an end in itself. It is only a servant of his dreams. Zarathustra must have known the secrets of cooking when he said:

> The body is my Great Reason. And an instrument of my body is my little reason, which you call 'spirit' – a little instrument and a toy of my Great Reason (*PN* 146).

The cook: a utopian being. He works in that space for the sake of another time and another space: those in which pleasure dwells. Chronology is reversed. The future is not a result of the present. It is the present, rather, which is made pregnant by the future.

A meal is the cook's soul transformed into food. So, as it is possible to interpret one's dreams, it is also possible to do a psychoanalysis of food. Every meal is a revelation, the dreams of the cook given to those who eat it: eucharist. And if we keep in mind Blake's remark that 'the Eternal Body of Man is The Imagination', we may as well conclude that it is the body of the cook which is eaten. 'Eat and drink, this is my body, this is my blood': anthropophagy.

But there is something else which is eaten with the food. As it is well known, cooks usually don't eat what they cook. They only taste it. Because cooks don't cook for themselves. They cook for others. The food is pleasurable, indeed. But they are after a higher joy; they eat something different. They eat the joy that they see in the other's face, as they eat. In that joy there is a silent love declaration. When the guests say 'How good it tastes!' they are also saying: 'How pleasurable are the dreams that live in the cook's body!' The cook eats with his eyes . . .

The food is being cooked on the stove. Unusual thoughts are also cooked in one's mind. 'What is cooking?' Our colloquial language knows that mind is a kitchen. Thinking is cooking; it is to transform raw ideas by the power of fire. And those thoughts which are prepared in the kitchen are different from those which abide in the classroom. In the classroom the eyes determine the etiquette to be obeyed. All ideas must be clear and distinct. The eyes leave the world untouched, because they are always distant and cannot do anything. In the kitchen another metaphysics is taught: the world is not there to be an object of contemplation; the world is to be eaten; it is to be transformed in a banquet. 'The great sorrow in human life, which begins in childhood and continues until death, is that seeing and eating are two different operations. To be real, it must be bodily, and to be bodily is to be eaten' (*LB* 167, 169).

The raw is 'reality' only in the absence of human bodies, when it has not yet been touched by the magic wand of desire. Once the human body becomes the centre of the universe, the raw becomes raw-material, mere possibility, nature in its dormant state, still improper to be eaten and in-corporated, unable to make love, the Sleeping Beauty, a strange, alien entity. There was one place only where stoves were not needed and nature could be eaten as it was: paradise. In paradise there were no altars, either. Altars, as it is well known, were places where the fire burned the meat. And God found pleasure in the 'soothing odour of the burnt offerings' (Gen. 8.20, 21). A curious idea keeps playing with me: that Abel offered the cooked and Cain offered the raw . . .

Philosophers, from time immemorial, have inquired about the 'foundations' of reality, the real substance of things, the immut-able which was hidden under the endless play of appearances. And some arrived at the conclusion that, in the last instance, water, earth, fire and air were everything which really existed. They were what was real. I can think of a philosopher, in earnest about his metaphysics who, having been invited to a banquet, complimented the hostess at the end, saying: 'Water, air, fire and earth were really delicious . . .' I imagine that he was never invited again. He was a creature of the classroom, who knew nothing about the metaphysics of eating. For him reality was the raw. He looked for what was in the beginning, before the kitchen had done its work, the 'arche'. But reality, for the cook (and also for Hegel . . .) is to be found at the end. This is the wisdom of body, the wisdom of desire: the world is destined to become a meal. And the kitchen is only a tinny sacred place, an altar, where this liturgy is celebrated and this eschatology realized.

What makes the difference is that in the kitchen a more fundamental element is added, the element which is the origin of all others: hunger, desire. In another place we said that the body is a thin web of flesh woven around a void. When we cook the void becomes active: fire. Longing. It burns and transforms. And nature becomes different from what it originally was: the 'humanization of nature'.

For this to happen the kitchen must be a place of destruction. Knives are sharpened, in order to cut. Fire is lit, in order to boil and burn. If it is true that cooking joins together what nature has separated, it is also true that cooking puts asunder what is joined in nature. The raw must cease to exist for something different to appear. One must die first, in order to be resurrected. Baptism – being drowned in water – comes before the creation of a new life. When the soup boils in the pan something is ceasing to be as it was, for a new, delightful thing, to exist. The man had to be dead in order to be 'eaten' by the villagers. 'My flesh is meat, indeed, and my blood is drink, indeed. Except you eat my flesh and drink my blood you have no life in you' (John 6.55, 53).

Cooking,
alchemy,
the fire of the stove and the fire of desire transubstantiate the raw into a new substance,
and the body,
in the darkness where taste dwells,
reencounters its lost blessedness.
A new variation on the theme of paradise,
the child and the mother's breast:
life and pleasure are given in the same place . . .
Dieticians know nothing about this miracle. They are the cook's mortal enemies. For them food is only a means for life. I

was once invited to a dinner which was introduced by a long lecture on the part of the dietician who had programmed it. And he spoke about the foundations of that meal, the basic elements which were there, and he explained all the body's needs to remain alive. That was the essence of the meal, for him. And taste was only an accident which is added, as sugar which is mixed with bitter medicine. For a dietician the body belongs to the medical order. The cook, however, knows that the body belongs to the order of love. We are what we eat. But we don't live by bread alone. Our heart longs for the erotic exuberance of the body . . .

Cooking is a liturgical ritual. In it our original truth, our eternal search for happiness is reenacted: the 'pleasure principle' takes the 'reality principle' in its hands, burns it on an altar, and its 'soothing odour' and good taste make love with our body. Not dualism but dialectics. Reality – the raw – and fire don't remain in separate rooms. They are brought together, 'without confusion', and a new reality comes into being. Whenever the stove is lit, the myth about our origins and destiny is reenacted.

The raw is transubstantiated.

We are also transubstantiated.

When food is taken, the power of the kitchen is also taken inside our bodies. The disciples of Emmaus reported that they felt something burning inside, as they ate. Their eyes were opened, and they knew. Vision and knowledge come through eating. The body is resurrected through eating. This is the magic of fire: it conjures up our forgotten potencies of love, which lie dormant in regions too deep for words. Food enters into depths where our erotic exuberance exists in silence.

Eating is more than feeding: it has to do with remembrance. 'Eat and drink in remembrance . . .' But we do not remember what is buried in chronological time. The past is gone, forever; it is a time which no longer exists. The time of death, impotent . . . We remember only what is still present, and yet forgotten. Remembering is the awakening of what was sleeping, the resurrection of what had been buried. Feuerbach once said that when we know an object we know ourselves. The object is the sensible presence of what was alive in us as an absence. The taste of the food is our own taste. The pleasure we feel in eating is the pleasure which lies dormant in our bodies. As we eat, food gives its kiss to our 'Sleeping Pleasure': and we become alive, again . . .

Eating teaches the basic lessons of love.

Love is eating.

Eating exists in the dialectic of love and its obscure object. This was our first lesson, learned in the breast of our mothers. Pleasure is when love and its object meet.

To love is to eat.

To love is to give oneself to be eaten.

Every food is an aphrodisiac.

There is no love-making if there is no desire.

The inexhaustible variety of the eating pleasures awaken in our bodies the inexhaustible varieties of hunger. 'Blessed are the hungry.' Only those who are hungry have the power to make love. This is the magic food performs: it erotizes our bodies, it awakens the fire of desire, it lights our dreams, we are made hungrier than we were. Every meal is an 'aperitif'. Our desire is never satisfied. If our desire is satisfied, we stop being lovers . . .

Now we see the profound insight of those languages which refer to love-making as 'eating'. Indeed, they are the same thing: to take the other inside, to feel his or her taste, to show, in one's eyes, that the other is pleasurable; to allow oneself to be taken inside the other, to offer one's body as bread and wine, and to enjoy the supreme blessedness of seeing ourselves reflected inside the mirror as the other's eyes, as something delightful. Narcissus . . .

The Latin languages preserve an intuition which seems to be absent from English. Their words for 'knowledge' and 'taste' come from the same root. 'Sapere', in Latin, means both to 'know' and to 'have flavour'. In my language, 'saber' – to know, and 'sabor' – taste. Eating and knowing have the same origin. To know something is to feel its taste, what it does to my body. Things are nothing in themselves. Kant knew about this, although he could not arrive at the kitchen, because he did not trust the body. Reality is not rawness, the 'things-in-themselves'. Reality is the result of the alchemic transformation by fire, the food which is taken inside my body. Reality is this encounter between mouth and food, desire and its object. As Buber suggests in his philosophy, it is not here, it is not there: it is 'in-between'. But this 'in-between' is nameless. Pleasure cannot be described. It is not an object for the kind of knowledge which lives in the classroom. The end of epistemology. Epistemology has to do with a knowledge which exists only in the pain of separation, when subjects are eternally apart, only linked by the distance of sight. But when the eyes are closed and unable to see, and the mouth tastes the food, all doubts are gone. 'I eat, therefore I am.' 'Taste and see that the Lord is good' (Psalm 34.8): put the Lord inside your mouth (God is to be eaten!) and you will know how good his/her/its taste is. Again, a poetic violence: one sees through the mouth . . .

No explanations are needed.

Explanations destroyed the pleasure of my father-in-law . . .

Explanations destroy the fun of jokes, the beauty of music, the joy of love.

'What precisely do you have in mind?' This is the classical question to be expected from philosophers.

'I don't know what I have in mind . . . but my body tells me precisely that the food which I have in my mouth tastes good . . .'

Pleasure has no reasons. 'Die Rose ist ohne warum. Sie blühet weil sie blühet': the rose has no why's; it blossoms because it blossoms . . .

Food delivers pleasure magically, without words, without understanding, 'ex opere operato'. Mediaeval theologians understood that this was how sacraments operated: by the simple power of eating. One eats and one's body is resurrected. The joy which lay there, buried in the forgetfulness of the flesh, comes out of the grave. A fire burns inside, the body is possessed. Just like when one drinks: up to a certain point, we drink; after that point we are drunk. We are metamorphosed into the likeness of the food: we are what we eat.

The dead man: the raw.

But it was transformed by the fire of the villagers' imagination.

And they, themselves, were resurrected by participating in the anthropophagic ritual . . .

The body is a kitchen.

Without the fire which burns inside,

the fire of hunger,

   desire,

   longing,

   imagination,

there cannot be any hope of resurrection, because we are what we eat.

Chapter VI

POETRY AND MAGIC

Poetry is the absolute real. This is the core of my philosophy. The more poetic, the more true.

Novalis

Poetry is also an incomprehensible sister of magic.

Guimarães Rosa

I must tell you a story: 'Babette's Feast'. It was written by Isak Dinesen (*Ladies Home Journal*, June 1950) and became a marvellous movie.

A village, lost in Denmark's coast, surrounded by great solitude and the mystery of the sea. Religion, the centre of its life . . . A stern pastor taught them the way to heaven: all the earthly pleasures had to be abandoned. This lesson was silently written everywhere: in their eyes, in their voices, in their smiles, in their clothes, in their food. The pastor had two daughters. They were beautiful. Many men came from afar just to see them. And many fell in love . . . But it was hopeless. Once a young army officer. But the father said 'No! She is my right hand in God's work. How could I allow her to go?' Then, an opera singer, who had come from Paris, and wanted to marry the second daughter. But the father said 'No! She is my left hand in God's work. How could I allow her to go?'

Many years elapsed. Time did its work. The pastor died. People got old, and also the two daughters. But the village did not change. The same eyes, the same voices, the same clothes, the same smiles, the same food. No, something changed. They got bitter. Now there was resentment and envy everywhere.

It was a rainy night. The wind blew wild through the empty street. A shadow moved in the dark. A woman. A stranger. She knocked at the door of the old house, where the two sisters lived. 'Who could it be, at this time?' they asked. They opened the door. The woman handed them a letter. It had come from France. It was signed by the singer. He told a story. There had been a revolution. The husband and the son of that woman had been killed. And her own life was in danger. She needed a place to hide. The village and their house had come to his mind. Could they receive her? She was a good cook . . .

'But we are poor', they said. 'We cannot pay you.'

'I will work for free', Babette replied. This was her name.

So, Babette stayed . . . She learned to cook the kind of food they used to eat: bread, fish, milk, and their possible combinations. For fourteen years she did her work faithfully.

But she had not forgotten her country. One single tie, a very improbable tie, an almost imperceptible tie, remained: a friend, every year, would buy her a lottery ticket . . .

The time came for the celebration of the centennial of the pastor's birth. The community thought that a frugal meal would do. Meals in heaven are frugal too, spiritual things only being served.

And it happened that one day – Babette was doing her work in the kitchen – the mail arrived: a letter for her. The two sisters brought her the letter – and there they stayed, staring at her. After some seconds Babette showed them what the letter had brought: a cheque. She had won the lottery. And in a split second the two sisters realized that Babette was lost. They would be alone again . . .

'I never asked you anything', Babette said. 'This will be my first request. I want to prepare the meal for the celebration of your father's centennial, French style . . .'

And since one is not supposed to deny the first and last request of someone who is about to depart, they agreed.

During all those years of heavenly food Babette had not forgotten her dreams. It seems that during those fourteen years Babette had been eating a kind of food which could not be found in the village: an absent food, her dreams. A different fire had been burning inside her body. And now the time had arrived: her dreams would become reality.

The raw materials had to be brought from afar.

She travelled to a distant city to place her orders.

Now she could: by grace, by chance. She had money, she had power . . . In the past she had said: 'Thus it is . . .'; but now she could say: 'But thus it will be.' Her dreams were about to become reality.

The whole village stopped to see, in wonder, the procession

which marched on the streets carrying the things which had come from unknown lands: boxes of all kinds, birds in cages and even a gigantic live turtle. And they knew that they were not going to eat their usual food . . .

The sisters were frightened. Would this meal be a reversal of everything they had believed in? In that night one of them had a nightmare: Babette was a witch, and what she had in store for them was a witch's sabbat, a devilish orgy for the damnation of their souls. The sisters gathered the community and shared their fears. A solution was found. They would go to the meal and eat of everything. But – they swore – they would not feel the taste of anything. They would cheat the devil . . .

The great day finally arrived. The fire burned in the kitchen as never before. Babette moved around as a witch, knowing what she was doing. Her face shone.

The table was set. A white linen cloth, imported dishware, silver candlesticks, crystal glasses. The guests began to arrive. Among them, as a surprise, the army officer of former times, now a general: he had come to visit his old aunt. He was the only one to ignore the oath of not feeling pleasure in the food. And the banquet began.

Wines were followed by all kinds of exquisite foods. The general expressed his delight. The guests replied by talking about the coming snow storm or the words of their deceased spiritual leader. Then, the most exquisite of all: the quails . . .

'Impossible', said the general. 'This dish is only served in a Paris restaurant. I remember . . . I had been invited . . . When this dish was served my host, a French general, remarked:

"I have been in duel because of beautiful women for many times. But since I came to know the woman who invented this dish I realized that I had found the woman of my dreams. She knows the magic of producing joy through food . . ."

Yes, it is the same dish. I even remember its name: "cailles au sarcophage . . ."'

But as they were eating a metamorphosis was occurring. The magic of food was stronger than the ideas they had in their heads. And slowly, silently, 'ex opere operato', it performed an alchemic change in their bodies. Their eyes, their voices, their words, their gestures: they became filled with kindness and joy, and the sleeping beauty which lived forgotten inside them woke up from its sleep.

And they returned to their childhood. As they left the house they clasped their hands, in a great circle, and sang songs of long ago . . .

The two sisters could not believe the miracle. They rushed to the kitchen to tell Babette how much they would miss her.

'Miss me?' she replied. 'But I am not going to leave . . .'

'But you are rich now!', the sisters said.

'No', Babette said. 'I spent everything in this feast. The money I spent would be, indeed, the price of a meal for thirteen guests, in the restaurant I worked, in Paris . . .'

Poor Babette . . . For fourteen years she only cooked and ate mixtures of fish, flour and milk. She lived with the villagers. She looked like one of them. There was one difference only: she had not forgotten. 'What memory loves is eternal.' In her silence there were memories of past joys unknown to all others. And it would be useless to speak. They would not understand. Like Cinderella, amidst the ashes, she dreamed dreams nobody could dream. And this was her real food: old recipes, formulas for the production of pleasure. One does not live by bread alone, but from words which contain the memory of a lost happiness. She did not long for anything new or different. She longed only for the old . . . Indeed, it is impossible to long for the new. How could one long for something one does not know? For one to long for something, one must have had the joy of its possession first. And longing comes when it is lost . . . Love wants to repeat, to recover, in the future, a lost time. Love is a 'recherche du temps perdu'.

For fourteen years Babette ate her dreams mixed with longing. Till one day, by sheer grace, the miracle happened . . .

But our dreams are too big. A kitchen is a little space, too little for the whole universe to be transformed into food. Our great sorrow is that we cannot eat everything we see . . . The kitchen and the pleasure it produces are only a metaphor for the great transformation by fire, the cosmic resurrection of the dead, apocalypse: this is the meal we long for. Babette could go to the big city and order the things she needed, even if they had to be brought from foreign lands. But where shall we place our order?

We are what we eat, it is true. But not the whole truth. We are also the food we desire and cannot eat. We are hungry beings, eternally. This is why food was mixed with bitter herbs, in the Easter meal . . . And we mix our food with words: sacraments: something is missing. Every meal is nothing more than an 'aperitif'.

And our body, this little kitchen, becomes filled with foods that will never be cooked in the kitchen outside: dreams . . . The body is a utopian kitchen . . . Dreams are this: that which the body longs for and yet cannot be eaten. And the body becomes a phantasmal space where a 'bacchanalian orgy' is cooked in the fire of desire.

We are what we eat.

We eat what does not exist: dreams.

We are the dreams we eat.

Dreams are good to eat: food . . .

We are transformed by the food we eat.

We are transformed by our dreams.

We are transformed by what does not exist.

'What are we without the help of that which does not exist?'

A dream is not a cogent argument.

A dream is not a true statement about reality outside.

It is not a convincing explanation.

It is not a chain of clear and distinct ideas, either.

Arguments have no taste,

explanations have no odour,

clear and distinct ideas don't have colours . . .

Dreams are not made up with ideas. They are made with images.

Images are the presence of the lost object of desire, offered to our senses. They invoke its erotic exuberance: colours, scents, tastes, touches. And the body makes love with the absent and experiences its delight, eschatologically.

All lovers know what I mean.

The fox smiled when she saw the wheat fields . . .

The disciples remembered a face as they ate bread and drank wine . . .

The lover cries or smiles as he or she sees the photograph of the beloved person . . .

Malinowski, in his description of magic, says that the person, refusing to accept the loss of the loved object, brings it inside his or her own body. It becomes, then, alive and the body is possessed by it (*MSR* 79–90). The body becomes an eschatological entity: in it the future is made present. The body brings together what time and space have separated. Indeed, as psychoanalysis has realized, in the unconscious there is neither time or space. What is dead and lost is brought back to life again.

Poets have, for long, recognized their kinship with magicians. 'Poetry is metamorphosis, transformation, alchemic operation', says Octávio Paz, 'and for this reason it lives close to magic and religion' (*AL* 137). And Guimarães Rosa, the supreme magician of Brazilian literature, sees writing as an 'alchemic process. The writer must be an alchemist', he says. 'The alchemy of writing demands the heart's blood. For one to be a wizard of the word, for one to study the alchemy of the blood of the human heart, one must have been born in the immense empty spaces of solitude' (sertão) (*LV* 13).

The scandal of psychoanalysis is due to its kinship with witchcraft. It begins by recognizing that the symptom, the wound open in the patient's body, was not produced by anything physical. The suffering person was bewitched by words, evil words, which now possess his or her body: demons. Neurosis and psychosis are witchcraft, black magic. And healing comes also through magic. 'Words and magic were, in the beginning, the same thing', says Freud (*GIP* 450). The psychoanalyst hears in silence in order to learn the name which keeps the body under its spell. 'What is your name?' – he asks. Because he knows that when their names are heard the evil spirits run away. As Fairbairn puts it, 'the psychotherapist is the true successor of the exorcist. His mission is not to forgive sins but to cast out demons' (*EPP* 56). Paraphrasing Wittgenstein, the analyst is involved in a 'battle against the bewitchment' which certain words have cast on us.

Poets have known the secret of magic. They deal with words as magical entities. Emily Dickinson gives the best description I know of the magical power of poetry:

> If I read a book and it makes my whole body so cold no fire can warm me, I know *that* is poetry. If I feel physically as if the top of my head were taken off, I know *that* is poetry. These are the only ways to know it. Is there any other way? (*FH* x).

Poetry is the language of what is not possible to say. It says without saying: metaphors . . . What the poem says is not present in its words. Indeed, the poet does not know what he is (not) saying. Like the empty hands in shell: they can hold water in their void, but they know nothing about water. Poetry says without saying. Paradox.

Everything is said in this marvellous poem, by Fernando Pessoa:

> Stop your singing!
> Stop, because,
> as I heard it,
> I heard also
> another voice
> coming from the interstices
> of the gentle enchantment
> which your singing
> brought unto us.
>
> I heard you
> and I heard it
> at the same time
> and different
> singing together.
> And the melody
> which was not there
> if I well remember
> makes me cry.

Your voice:
was it an enchantment which,
unwillingly,
in this vague moment
woke up
a certain being
to us a stranger
which spoke to us?

I don't know. Don't sing.
Let me hear
the silence
that there is
after your singing.

Oh! Nothing, nothing!
Only the sorrow
for having heard,
for having wished to hear
beyond the meaning
that a voice has.

Which angel, as you spoke,
without your knowledge
came down to earth
where the soul wanders
and with his wings
blew the embers
of an unknown home?

Stop your singing!
I wish the silence
to put to sleep
the memory
of the voice I heard,
misunderstood,
which was lost
as I heard it (*PFP* 202).

[97]

Two melodies . . .

The one I hear: it comes with yours words, your voice . . .

The other, which is not yours, was heard in the interstices of your words, out of your silence. Yes, I heard the two of them at the same time. But they did not say the same thing: they were different. And what is amazing is that it was not your singing, but the melody which was not there which made me cry. I don't know what it says. Indeed, I tried 'to go beyond the meaning that a voice has'. The name of the singer who sang the melody which was not there? I don't know. It is not me. It is not you. A Stranger, certainly an Angel who, coming from another world, 'with his wings blew the embers of an unknown home . . .'. 'We see what we had already seen. We feel as if we return, we hear again, we remember . . .' (*AL* 211). From our exile, this land where the soul wanders, we return to our home: we see again our truth, our origin and destiny.

Truth appears as we stumble, when the frozen surface of the lake cracks and we hear its voice: dreaming . . .

We are saved by the power of dreaming. Dreaming is the power which resurrects the dead.

The dead man in the village: a word with no meaning in it; a silent word. Was he the Angel who 'with his wings blew the embers of an unknown home'?

Babette also had nothing to say. She only prepared a meal, and as they ate the bewitchment was broken: and they played as children: the lost time returned . . .

So the eucharist: an empty, silent space for our dreaming, before the Absent One – like the dead man of the sea . . .

It is not the presence which performs the miracle. The miracle is performed by the power of the absence.

God is the absence which saves. As Riobaldo, the rustic hero of Guimarēs Rosa, puts it, 'God exists even when he is not' (*GSV* 49). And our theme is heard again:

'What are we without the help of that which does not exist?'

It is not theology.

Theology wants to be science, a discourse without interstices . . .

It wants to have its birds in cages . . .

Theopoetics instead,

empty cages,

word which are uttered out of and before the void,

the deep sea (and the eyes look upward, waiting for the light which fractures through unquiet waters . . .),

deep forest (if one has patience one will hear the voice of an enchanted bird who lives there – and yet it has never been seen by anyone . . .),

empty cathedral, where our thoughts become light and jump over abysses . . .

Exegetes and hermeneuts are at a loss.

Their job is to find the meaning that a voice *has*. They hear, they read and they say: 'This is the meaning of the words!' But now, if the poet is to be believed, 'there is another voice' which lives in the 'interstices': the silences of the text.

Could they, exegetes and hermeneuts, produce a science out of the void? The villagers produced a discourse out of the void; but it was not science; it was dreaming . . . No, definitely no. Exegetes and hermeneuts are forbidden to 'wish to hear beyond the meaning that a voice has'. They are not allowed to speak about a 'melody which is not there'. The members of the order remained at a critical distance from the dead man. 'Does this dead man really sing all these melodies?' Their painful scientific, historical, hermeneutical work had one purpose only: to determine, with precision, the meaning that that text had. Nothing more. Nothing less. Science. The meaning it *had*. The voices of silence cannot become the object of scientific knowledge. They are only (non) objects to poetry . . .

'What did the author have in mind?'

'What did he want to say?'

The writer failed. He wanted to say but he did not. Instead of 'clear and distinct ideas' he used the ambiguous symbols which made a mysterious text, filled with dubious and contradictory meanings: interstices.

Exegesis and hermeneutics come to help the poet out of his

speech disturbance. They will bring light into darkness. The meaning will be preserved and confusion dispelled.

A new, luminous text will be produced.

Poetry will become prose.

The Ego will bring its lights into the caves of the Id.

Poetry: one single word pregnant with unpredictable meanings. Do you remember? 'As I heard it I heard also another voice coming from the interstices . . .'

Prose: many words to say one 'single, simple, solid and stable meaning'.

Poetry: one word which leads to infinite horizons.

Prose: many words which are a funnel which leads to one single, precise meaning.

In poetry one does not know what one is talking about.

Prose is the opposite: one knows what one is talking about.

Prose is knowledge.

And poetry? what is it?

> A poem should be palpable
> and mute
> as a globed fruit

says Archibald McLeish.

> A poem should be wordless
> as the flight of birds.
> A poem should not mean
> but be . . .

And E. E. Cummings agrees:

> Poetry is being, not doing (*SNL* 24).

'The image', says Gaston Bachelard, 'does not demand any knowledge. The poetic image is not an echo of the past. It is rather the reverse: by the explosion of the image, a far away past reverberates in echoes . . .' (*DS* xxvi).

A poem is like a Gothic cathedral.

What is its meaning?

What did the architect have in mind?

Indeed, it is possible to do a psychological, biographical, historical investigation in order to find the answer to these questions. This was what the members of the monastic order did.

But these questions have little to do with the magical power of the cathedral. Magical powers don't abide in the past. They belong to the present, where life is happening. The cathedral: its vast, empty spaces, its silence, the light which fractures through iridescent glasses, the darkness which plays with the dance of the candles and gives movement to the stones . . . Yes, the cathedral is like the dead man: it is filled with unspoken words, filled with unexpected worlds . . . In it lives a Stranger – not the architect and his meanings – and when this Stranger speaks, one hears far away bells tolling inside one's soul: and the body trembles . . . Is the cathedral outside a metaphor of the cathedral inside? Or is it the other way round? I don't know – and the memory of an unknown home comes back to me. My knowledge fails me in that moment, I don't need it – I am possessed by the Wind which moves in the Void.

'What did you want to say', the interpreter asks the poet.

And the poet replies:

'I wanted to say precisely what I said.'

There is no way of improving a poem.

None of its words can be exchanged by a synonym.

As with the cathedral, its darkness cannot be exchanged for light, its silence for words.

'What I said is precisely what I wanted to say because this is what I saw', says the poet. I saw the light which fractures through unquiet waters. I am a submarine being. My eyes indeed are two dim fishes in the deep of the sea, surrounded by silence and darkness. And I also hear the voice of the lovely, dark and deep woods, seducing me . . . Please, don't empty the sea in order to see better. I am a submarine entity, my eyes are fishes . . . If you empty the sea, I will die. And don't bring lights inside the woods, in order to get rid of the night. Because if you do this, the woods will stop singing . . .

Mediaeval theologians, specially the mystical, were fully aware of the poetical nature of the Sacred Name. Scotus Erigena compared it to the iridescent colours of the peacock's feathers: one single feather, many colours which shine and mingle. Every word is filled with f/lights beyond our control. In prose we *have* the word: birds in cages. In poetry the words explode the cage in which they were trapped, and they fly and take us on their wings.

But it is precisely this freedom of the poetic word which frightens power. The Great Inquisitor condemned the Word to death in order to keep his many words in jail. Inquisitors always condemn the Word to silence . . .

Protestant theology was born when the magical-poetic power of the Word was rediscovered
and democratized.

Every individual was to read the scriptures as one reads a poem, alone, without any intervening voices of interpretation. Hermeneuts were to be silent, so that the believer could hear the voice of the Stranger: the inner testimony of the Holy Spirit. It was believed that the forgotten words written in the flesh and the Word coming from the past would meet and make love – and the miracle would happen. If, by sheer grace, the Wind blew and the melody which was not there was heard, the dead would be resurrected.

But soon the demands of power realized that the freedom of the Wind is dangerous, because it blows where and how it wills. So, they tried to domesticate it and flying birds were put inside word-cages:

images became dogmas,

metaphors were transformed into doctrines,

poetry was rewritten as 'confessions',

the pregnant silence before the Void became demands of understanding,

and the disturbing mystery of the Gothic cathedral gave place to the full luminosity of the Calvinistic temple: a classroom. But in classrooms there is no silence, except the silence to hear the voice of another, the sermon. As opposed to the untamable freedom of the poetic word, Protestantism inaugurated the hermeneutical program which, in the end, implies the filling of all empty spaces, the only spaces where the voice of the Stranger can be heard. In Luther's own words, the task of interpretation is to determine the 'unum, simplicem, solidum et constantem sensum' (*LB* 192), the 'single, simple, solid and stable meaning' of the scripture. The 'crux is the reduction of meaning to one single meaning', the transformation of poetry into prose: the beginning of scientific theology (*LB* 214).

Once the work is accomplished, once all the gaps are filled by knowledge, we discover that the Word has lost the power to resurrect the dead.

The body is not moved by what is said and known, but by what remains unspoken and silent. Word and flesh make love in the interstices, there where our dreams dwell. Bachelard's words come to my mind: 'one does not persuade except by suggesting the fundamental dreams, except by restoring to thought its avenues of dreaming' (*DS* xxiv). As A. Govinda put it, in his study of Tibetan mysticism, people are converted 'through that which goes beyond words and flows directly from the presence of the saint: the inaudible mantric sound that emanates from his heart' (*FTM* 226).

As it happened in the village . . .

Chapter VII

BEAUTY AND POLITICS

Conseille, ô mon rêve,
que faire?

Mallarmé

What was an inner light becomes a
consuming fire that spreads outward.

Karl Marx

Both Freud and Marx foretold the end of religion. But for opposite reasons.

Freud knew the secrets of the human heart and was aware of the size of our dreams: they are too big. So big that, for them to be fulfilled, we would have to be gods. But gods we are not. We are human beings: our hands are weak. They do not have power enough to create the objects of our desire. We are Babette, during the fourteen years of her longing. The dream of the banquet: she had it. But the kitchen was empty. So, she had to get used to fish soup and bread. This modest meal was all that reality permitted. Paradise was lost, forever . . . Paraphrasing Marx' words Freud would say that 'psychoanalysis has plucked the imaginary flowers from the chain so that we will wear the chain without any fantasy or consolation, since we will not be able to shake off the chain and cull the living flower'. Reality is the chain, a stern stoic teacher who teaches us the wisdom of abandoning our impossible desires. The raw will remain raw. No banquet will be served. Religion is an illusion which is doomed to disappear.

Marx also spoke in the name of reality. But reality, for him, was not the chain, but the hands which make and break the chain. Reality is not what the past has bequeathed us but rather what the hands can do. He was sure that hearts, heads and hands, together, would steal the Garden of Delights from the domain of gods, where religious fantasies had exiled it, so that a real garden could be planted in the world. The chains would be broken. We would no longer need any 'fantasy or consolation' because by means of politics we would 'cull the living flower'. Paradise would be regained. Happiness would return. And religion would wither away. Why should one dream about Paradise if one is living in it? For what is religion? Religion is the 'sigh of the oppressed creature' as it wanders, exiled, on this 'vale of woe', a long way from home (*OR* 42). When the beloved person is absent one writes letters. But when she or he returns, letters become meaningless. Instead of letters, which are words written in the pain of absence, the love embrace . . . Happiness puts an end to all transcendent fantasies. Now we are like Babette, after she was hit by grace and won the lottery: the banquet is served. Instead of dreaming, eating . . . Paradise returns, religion departs. And the sacred texts agree: in Paradise there are no altars, as in the Holy City there are no temples . . .

Marx, as opposed to Freud, was optimistic. Psychoanalysis believes that our desire is a wound which cannot be healed. Our desire is rooted in a tragedy which antecedes history, where our hands cannot go. In this it resembles the doctrine of the original sin: our bodies are born with a Void inside that nothing can fill. Marx, on the contrary, believed that our tragedy was born in time. It is a historical accident and not a metaphysical necessity. If desire is exiled from Paradise it is because we have exiled it. We are guilty of this deed, and our past history tells the story of this tragedy. And because we are guilty, there is hope. The hand which inflicted the wound has the power to heal it. History is what we have done by means of our acts – praxis – and whatever we had the power to do we have also the power to undo.

Praxis: what we do with our hands: this is the key to Paradise. For Paradise to return our desire must not be bigger than our hands. Dreams grow out of impotent hands. When the hands are powerless, they dream . . . Thus, the obscure mystery of the heart is resolved in the clear, scientific knowledge, of what our hands can do. Dreams no longer need to be interpreted because they are not the locus where our riddle is revealed. Dreams are nothing more than reversed images of our impotence, inside a mirror. Why should we look at the mirror if the original is directly accessible to scientific investigation? As Marx himself put it, 'all mysteries which mislead theory to mysticism find their rational solution in the human praxis and in the comprehension of this praxis' (*OR* 71).

Power is the key which makes it possible to decypher the riddle of the human world, just as mathematics is the key to decypher the riddle of the physical world. And just as the physicist must refrain from speaking about his feelings, for the sake of true knowledge, so the person who wants to understand history must refrain from speaking about the mystical halo which envelops it: our religious dreams.

There are no mysteries: we act out of power and not out of our dreams.

Marx describes politics, as it really happens. It is a fact that love has been proscribed by power. As Berdyaev once put it in a poetical way, 'the politician and the sergeant major, the banker and the lawyer, are stronger than the poet and the philosopher, the prophet and the saint. The Son of God was crucified. Socrates was poisoned. The prophets were stoned' (*SF* 67).

Politicians, indeed, just like business men, their twin-brothers, never speak about love. If they do, one must be sure that they are talking about something else. Love is never the source or the end of what they do. Love is always a means to power. The love-bait has always an iron hook hidden inside.

The end of religion? No. The advent of a new religion. Power now takes the place of religion as it promises to fulfill its dreams. One no longer needs to speak about love because it is believed that power will produce what it longs for. The limits of the hands denote the limits of the heart. The heart is reduced to hands. We desire only what our hands can give. The riddle of love is solved. If the mystery of religion is the mystery of desire, and if the mystery of desire is resolved as power, power becomes the new religion. As Camus once said, 'Marx only understood that a religion which did not embrace transcendence should properly be called politics' (*R* 196). But, as in the parable of the empty house (Luke 11.24), the empty space left by one evil spirit is filled by seven spirits, worse than the former. The place of the forgotten dream is taken by the illusion of power: that our hands can produce what the heart demands.

The prophets denounced this illusion and called it 'idolatry'. An idol is a man-made object which is trusted as having the power to bring back happiness.

Theologians named it 'justification by works': the riddle of our desires is solved by means of our action.

And the mythical stories described it as 'demonic possession'. Luke 5 tells the story of a man who was filled with power. So strong he was that he wrenched apart all the chains and fetters with which he had been bound. But this power did not make him happy. He lived with the dead, among the tombs. And night and day, from the sepulchres and on the mountains, he cried and cut himself with stones. The Devil had kept his promise. He had given him power in exchange for love. And because the memory of love had been robbed from him, his power was unable to create anything which could give him pleasure. The power of love produces beauty and happiness. But the love of power can only produce pain and death. And if power without love is the Devil, we come to the conclusion that there is something demonic in the realm of politics. Indeed, the highest expressions of the political order are nothing but the triumph of power over love.

'Robberies: what are they but little kingdoms?', says Augustine. 'The band itself is made up of men; it is ruled by the authority of a prince, it is knit together by the pact of a confederacy; the booty is divided by the law agreed on. If, by the admittance of abandoned men, this evil increases to such a degree that it holds places, fixes abodes, takes possession of cities, and subdues peoples, it assumes more plainly the name of a kingdom, because the reality is now manifestly conferred on it, not by the removal of covetousness, but by the addition of impunity' (*CG* 113).

When Augustine defined the state as a successful robbery, he was saying that its essence is not the happiness it promises to produce but rather the power it holds with impunity. Many centuries after, Max Weber almost repeated Augustine's words. 'The State', he says, 'is a human community that (successfully) claims the monopoly of the legitimate use of physical force within a given territory.' But the word 'legitimate' has no relation to love and justice, since the state 'is considered the sole source of the "right" to use violence.' 'Every State', said Trotsky, 'is founded on force' (*MW* 78).

No wonder that Nietzsche called it 'the coldest of all cold monsters'. 'Behold', he says, 'how the State lures them, the all-too-many – and how it devours them, chews them, and ruminates! "On earth there is nothing greater than I: the ordering finger of God am I" – thus roars the monster. And it is not only the long-eared and short-sighted who sink to their knees. Alas, to you too, great souls, it whispers its dark lies. You have grown weary with fighting, and now your weariness still serves the new idol. With heroes and honourable men it would surround itself, the new idol! It will give you everything if you will adore it, this new idol: thus it buys the splendour of your virtues and the look of your proud eyes. It would use you as a bait for the all-too-many. Indeed, a hellish artifice was invented there, a horse of death, clattering in the finery of divine honours. Indeed, a dying for many was invented there, which praises itself as life: verily, a great service to all preachers of death. State I call it where all drink poison; State, where the slow suicide of all is called life' (*PN* 162).

The state, indeed, is born when all sell their souls to Leviathan. And whenever our soul is sold, the Devil takes hold of our bodies.

Nicolas Berdyaev is of the same opinion.

> The weird and horrible phenomenon of human life which today is called the totalitarian state, is certainly not a temporary and accidental phenomenon of a certain epoch. It is the revelation of the true nature of the state. That which has been considered immoral for a person has been considered entirely moral for the state. The state has always used evil means – espionage, falsehood, violence, murder; there have been distinctions in this respect in degree only; these methods, indisputably very evil, have always been justified by a good and exalted view in end. For the sake of the majesty of the state and the prestige of authority they have tortured individual men and women and whole nations. The state has respected the rights of man less than

anybody. Politics are always an expression of the slavery of man (*SF* 140, 142, 143, 149).

No, it is not that evil men make politics. The truth is that the seduction of power buys the soul even of the best, and at the end they are all prisoners of the iron logic of power. Power performs the evil magic of transforming dreamers into individuals to be used and administrated, so that the 'reasons of the state' – which are the reasons of power – will triumph. The state transforms the resurrection of the dead into the administration of the living ones. And as this takes place, the living ones become the valley of dry bones (Ezek. 37). The state is prophecy in reverse. Many are the languages it speaks: order, progress, security, prosperity, brotherhood and even freedom. But they all mean the same thing: 'All these things I will give you, if you fall down and worship me.'

The end of religion does not come alone. It is the end of all dreaming. In *1984* to dream was a crime, because dreaming bears witness to the fact that the state has not fulfilled its promises.

Nietzsche foretold this possibility with horror, and spoke about the time when 'man will no longer shoot the arrow of his longing beyond man, and the string of his bow will have forgotten how to whirl! The time is coming when man will no longer give birth to a star!' (*PN* 129)

Karl Mannheim – a social scientist who knew that the soul of the human world is dreaming – also foresaw this day with great sorrow. 'It is possible,' he says, 'that in the future, in a world in which nothing new happens' (like the village, before the gift of the sea), 'in which everything will be terminated and each moment will be the repetition of the past, there will be a condition in which thought will be totally void of ideological and utopian elements.' (No kitchen: we will eat the raw . . .) 'But this condition, in which all transcendent elements of reality are eliminated, in our world, leads to an objectivism which, in the last instance, implies the dissolution of the human will . . . human beings themselves will be transformed into things. We would be then confronted with the greatest imaginable paradox: man, having attained the

[111]

highest degree of rational domination of his existence, is abandoned by all ideal, becoming then nothing more than a plaything at the mercy of the impulses. So, at the end of a long, tortuous but heroic development, with the abandonment of utopias, man looses the will to shape history and, with it, the capacity to understand it' (*IU* 244). Politics will then cease to be the art of making the future present, and will become the science of the administration of the existing order. We will be, then, as in Eliot's poem, 'the hollow people'.

But this is what the Devil is all about. In his commentary on the Epistle to the Romans Barth wrote:

> Is not the existing order a reinforcement of men against God, a safeguard of the normal course of this world against the disturbance by the great ambiguity and its defense against the pre-supposition by which it is threatened on all sides? Are not the ordinances of men simply a conspiracy of the Many against the One? *Rulers!* What are rulers but men? What are they but men hypocritically engaged in setting things in order, in order that they ensure themselves securely against the riddle of their own existence? Men have no right to possess objective right against other men. Is there anywhere authority which is not ultimately based upon tyranny? (*ER* 478).

Poets are among the few who perceive the farce. They show that the king is naked . . . This is why power has always tried to domesticate the poets. 'The modern political parties', says Octávio Paz, 'have transformed the poet into a propagandist. The propagandist disseminates among the "masses" the conceptions of the hierarchs. His task is to transmit certain directives, from the top to the bottom' (*AL* 50). It seems that this was one of the reasons which lead Maikovski to commit suicide. The party demanded that he used poetry as a means to inculcate ideology, whereas his soul was committed to beauty. One understands, then, the bitter judgment that Guimarães Rosa passes on politicians. 'As opposed to the professional politicians I believe in man and wish him a future. I am a writer. I think about eternities. The politician thinks only about minutes. I think about the resurrection of man' (*LV* 10).

But this denunciation is followed by hope. 'Maybe I am a politician', he adds. Of a different kind. He wants to change the world through the power of the poetical word. 'It is only by the renewal of the word that the world can be renewed', he says. The poet follows the opposite direction of normal politics. 'The poet operates from the bottom up: from the language of his community to the language of the poem. His word, then, returns to its sources and becomes an object of communion' (*AL* 50). 'Regeneration of Language', says Eugen Rosenstock-Huessy, 'would be no faulty name for the due process of revolution' (*OoR* 739). Poetry reveals, then, what it is: 'Knowledge, salvation, power, abandonment – an operation capable of transforming the world . . . The poetic operation is revolutionary by nature . . . Poetry reveals this world and creates another' (*AL* 15).

A politics out of poetry? It is rather strange. Because politics has to do with crowds, whereas the poetic experience grows out of solitude. 'Works of art are of an infinite loneliness', says Rilke. They are not produced democratically. They grow silently, inside the artist's body. As opposed to the politicians, who cannot survive without the party and public opinion, the artist lives in a special world the centre of which is his own body. 'Every artist's strictly illimitable country is himself', says E. E. Cummings. He might speak about universes and eternities, but everything grows out of his longing. He is 'a thinking mirror of the universe' (*FP* 144). 'The stars', says Álvaro de Campos, 'I took them out of my pocket. In me all the forces of the universe are reflected' (*PAC* 113). The artist's fundamental dream is the same dream of the child because, as Ferenczi suggested, our original symbols are expressions of our desire of finding our whole body in the universe (*MK* 91).

But the artist knows that this is only a dream. He is the only one to feel and see it. He is surrounded by a great solitude. This is why beauty is always mixed with sadness.

As I write I hear Beethoven's 'Hammerklavier' sonata. And, in spite of its overwhelming beauty, I feel a gentle sadness moving inside my soul.

'In spite of' or 'because of'?

'Because the sky is blue it makes me cry . . .'

It is easy not to cry: one should beware of looking at the blue skies, one should no longer hear the sonata . . .

But there is no way out: if one wants the supreme joy of beauty, one must be prepared to cry. Sadness is not an intruder in beauty's domains. It is rather the air without which it dies. Artists are always sad. Alberto Caeiro says that he is 'sad as a sunset' and Vinícius de Moraes confessed that he always felt like crying before beauty.

Beauty is sad because beauty is longing. The soul returns to one's lost home. And the return to the 'no longer' is always painful. The sunset, the blue skies, the sonata: they are there, but they are not our possession. Elusive like the sunset, the blue skies, the sonata, beauty touches us and quickly goes leaving only nostalgia in its place. Like God . . .

And yet we want it again. We want to cry. Is there any 'pleasure' in crying? Freud suggested that the fundamental force which moves our soul is the principle of pleasure. I would suggest that, maybe, it is the 'principle of beauty' . . . We want to return to beauty, because of the (sad) love story which it tells; because it is the place of our truth: our lost home . . .

'O, Lord! That there not be so much beauty!', exclaims Rafael Cansinos-Assés, the Jewish–Spanish poet. Beauty makes us remember . . . We remember that we are exiles. We remember that the object of our longing has either not yet arrived or has gone away. We remember that we are utopian beings, with no solid ground under our feet. Beauty uproots us from the solid realities of our daily lives, the 'reality principle', the home of normal politics, and we find ourselves loose in the air, alone, lost. 'When we feel most safe something happens: a sunset, the end of a Euripedes' choir, and we are lost again . . .' (*SN* 136, 137).

Beauty is what love does 'in absentia'; it is
'to fix the room for the dead son' (Chico Buarque).
The spider: I remember it.
Her body rests on the cobweb she has woven.
She feels safe, on good grounds: the threads of her cobweb are
securely tied around the branches of a tree. She would be a good,
realist politician . . .
Artists are not that lucky. They also weave webs. But they are
not tied around any solid ground. Their cobwebs look more like
wings which grow out of their bodies. They are not anchored in
anything. They float. They 'are swimmers in a buoyant and
everlasting medium' (*OoR* 750).
Beauty is full of love
but void of power.
The artist's hands are empty.
What he has: symbols in his mouth . . .
But they are not enough . . .
'Symbols?'
I am fed up with symbols', says Álvaro de Campos.
'I am told that everything is symbol.
Which symbols?
Dreams . . .
But I don't want symbols . . .
I want (what a poor word for poverty and helplessness . . .)
that the lover returns to the girl who waits for him' (*PAC* 68).
The poem is a wingless arrow which wants to fly.
And the arrow prays for the bow.
This is the secret of life, the secret of our bodies.
Life is always 'will to power', said Nietzsche.
Every poem is an incantation, a prayer, an invocation of
power. The poet waits for the One who will have beauty in his
heart and power in his hands: gracious power . . . The biblical
tradition calls him by the name of Messiah. The Messiah is the
symbol for this miraculous event: the ephemeral coincident
between love and power: when the Lion, as in Zarathustra's
parable, makes room for the Child, and disappears (*PN* 139).

Ephemeral because it is grace. It cannot be institutionalized as a party, a state, a church. It takes on visible form as a people.

A people? What is this? Augustine suggests:

'A people is an assemblage of reasonable beings bound together by a common agreement as to the objects of their love' (*CG* 706).

Those who have the same dreams.

It is out of the dreams which live in the hearts of the people that gardens grow, because 'better worlds are born, not made' (*SNL* 31).

There are two sorts of politics.

By the love of power the people become playthings, objects, at the mercy of those who have power. They are forced to forget their dreams. They die.

By the power of love – the politics of beauty – a people is born and deserts become gardens.

Vinicius de Moraes, who wrote 'The Girl from Ipanema', describes this miraculous event in his poem 'The Worker in Construction'.

> He it was who built houses
> where before was empty land.
> Like a bird with no wings
> he flew as high as the buildings
> that sprouted from his hand.
> But he ignored everything
> of his great mission.
> He did not know, for example,
> that a house is a temple,
> a temple without religion.
> Nor did he know
> that the house he was building
> instead of being his freedom
> would indeed become his prison.
>
> Indeed, how could
> a humble brick-layer

understand why a brick
should be worth more than bread?
Bricks he placed one on the top of the other
with trowel, cement and square.
As for bread, he could eat it!
But imagine eating a brick!
So the worker continued
with sweat and cement
building one house here,
there an apartment.
A church, a barracks, a prison:
a prison that would have been meant for him
were he not a worker in construction.

But it happened one day
at the table, while cutting his bread,
the worker was invaded
by a sudden emotion
as he discovered, astonished,
that everything on the table,
plate, knife and bottle –
they were all made by him,
a humble worker in construction.

He looked around:
bench, pellet, window,
house, city and nation!
Everything that existed
was made by him,
a humble worker
who knew how to exercise his profession.

Ah, men of knowledge!
You will never know the magnitude
of what dawned upon the worker
at that moment!
In that empty house

he had built himself,
a new world was born . . .
And in excitement the worker
looked at his hands,
his rough hands of a worker,
and had in a moment the impression
that nothing in the world,
was more beautiful than them.

It was in the understanding
of this solitary moment
that like the houses he built
the worker himself grew.
He grew in height and in depth,
in breadth and in his heart.
And the worker acquired a dimension which was new,
the dimension of poetry.

And a new fact was seen:
what the worker was saying
by the others was heard.
And so it was that the worker
who had always said 'yes'
began to say 'no' (*VAP* 205).

It is a long poem which cannot be reproduced here in full. But what interests us is this magical leap when the worker, by the power of poetry, gained new eyes, and everything became different.

He was eating – like the disciples of Emmaus.

Suddenly, the transfiguration of everything.

Nothing was changed – the same bricks, the same walls, the same objects . . . And yet, there was a different light. Everything became transparent and he saw things which he had never seen. Knowledge would not have performed the miracle. It was something, burning inside. And out of those old and tired objects, beauty appeared. The worker was possessed by it. He was a new creature. And, from his mouth, the word which had remained forgotten, unspoken, inside of his body, the word which would be the beginning of a new world . . . He spoke as a poet – and then, the miracle of communion. They were all conspirers. They knew what their dreams were. And they said: 'No'.

I remember.

It was during the darkest days of repression in Brazil.

Torture chambers were filled with the bodies of the victims. Fear was mixed with the air. There was a poet, Geraldo Vandre. He wrote a song:

> Walking and singing
> and following the song:
> we are all equals,
> we are all brothers . . .

Such simple words. But they expressed the truth of our forbidden dreams: the departure of fear, the return of beauty, people marching together, following the song . . . The next day it was heard everywhere: on the streets, on the markets, in the radios. It had become a sacrament of conspiracy. No, the people was not dead. It was only sleeping.

Power became frightened. It does not know what to do with beauty. It is easy to deal with power. One simply uses more power. A machine gun against a rifle . . . But how could the cages of repression encage the wind? Does it not move wild as the poetic word? I remember Luther saying in one of his 'Table Talks' that the Reformation had not been done by the power of the hands, but by the power of the word. Indeed, he remarked jokingly, 'as I and Melanchthon drink beer the word moves freely through the country . . .'

The future abides in the poetic word.

This is the dwelling place of the absent, by whose power we are saved . . .

Utopias: never to be reached, like the stars. But how sad the night would be, without them! And how could the lost sailors find their way? According to a very old story, one must follow the unreachable star if one is to find the place where the Messiah has been born . . .

I transcribe this paragraph in which Ernst Bloch illuminates the utopian contents of beauty:

> If things are commonly seen as they are
> it is not uncommonly paradoxical to put at least as much trust in their ability to be other than they are. Therefore, Oscar Wilde's remark about a map of the world without the land of Utopia not being worth a glance evokes no shock but the shock of recognition.
>
> True, things themselves offer only a dotted line of extension to something like that land; but all the world's positivists could not erase it from what really is so.
>
> Every work of art which represents and informs this possibility is full of augmented horizon problems . . . Therefore great works of art can dispense least of all with the creative touch of poetic anticipation – the pre-semblance of what, objectively, is still latent in the world. In the great works of art the self-light of this utopian presence glows on the horizon. In a work of art sorrow and anguish never remain unilluminad, just as they are; and joy always dawn as a fore-glow . . . Schiller's 'Ode to Joy' shines beyond what has been experienced hitherto because it already names and summons perfect joy . . . (*PF* 96–98).

Thus lives the warrior, born out of visions of beauty:
with one eye he sees darkness and pain,
but with the other he sees light and joy.

The warrior is a body which has heard the voice of the poet, has been possessed by beauty, and flies like the arrow into the future by virtue of the bow of power. In him, in Marx' words, 'what was an inner light becomes a consuming flame that spreads outwards' (*MHO* 19).

And, as he flies, his song is heard:

Wake and listen,
you that are lonely!
From the future come winds with secret wing-beats; and
    good-tidings are proclaimed to delicate ears.
You that are lonely,
you that are withdrawing,
you shall, one day,
be the people.
Out of you shall grow a chosen people.
Verily the earth shall yet become a site of recovery.
And even now a new fragrance surrounds it, bringing
    salvation
and a new hope (*PN* 189).

Chapter VIII

PROPHECY

Prophesy to the Wind, prophesy, man,
and say to it:
These are the words of the Lord God:
Come, O Wind,
come from every quarter
and breathe into these slain,
that they may come to life.
(Ezekiel 37.9)

And when we have built an altar
to the Invisible Light,
we may set thereon
the little lights
for which our bodily vision was made.
T. S. Eliot

My friend smiled and remarked that during the last twenty years I have been saying the same thing, all the time. His voice was soft and there was no criticism in it. It was as if he were saying: 'I finally understood you. I have heard the unspoken word which comes from the interstices of your ten thousand words . . .'

He was right. I feel that what I do with words is what musicians do with sounds: 'variations on a given theme'. I don't want to change my subject. Mallarmé is my brother: I want to write a book with one single word. And Kierkegaard's aphorism never abandons me: 'Purity of heart is to desire one thing only . . .'

Before I began playing this game with words I tried to play it with sounds. I wanted to be a pianist. But I failed. After much painful striving I realized that I did not have talent. So, I gave it up. But something of the musician's soul survived in me. Bach, Mozart, Beethoven, Brahms, Britten, Ravel, they all enjoyed composing 'variations on a given theme'. As opposed to the game of scientific truth, which comes to an end when one arrives at a definite statement of its vision, beauty always demands repetition. Beauty is infinite; it is never satisfied with a final form. Every experience of beauty is the beginning of a new universe. This is why the same theme must be repeated, every time in a different form. Every repetition is the resurrection of a past experience which must remain alive.

The same poem,
the same music,
the same story . . .

And yet, they are never the same, every time fresh, every time new . . .

The ecstasis of the contemplation of truth happens only once, 'apax'. It cannot be repeated. Every repetition is a disappointment, it has the flat taste of 'déjà vu'. The excitement of the first time is gone forever. But beauty is different. Every time it is repeated, the body reverberates again. The ecstasis of love always longs for its return . . .

If we are to believe in what poets say, this is so because our souls are like a canon, a perpetual fugue. Beauty is when this fugue is played again. 'This is how human life is composed', says Milan Kundera, 'like a musical score. The human being, guided by the sense of beauty, takes an accidental fragment and transforms it into a theme which will become part of the score of our lives. We will return to this theme, repeating, modifying, developing and transposing it, just as the composer does to the themes of his sonata. The human being unconsciously composes life's score according to the laws of beauty, even in the moments of deepest despair' (*ILS* 58).

'Unconsciously?' Yes. Without knowing, we know.

Psychoanalysis is an attempt to identify the theme which is always played as ten thousand variations. Let your thoughts dance as they please! Let images and words associate freely. It does not matter where the game begins. Sooner or later one will begin to hear the song of the 'Sleeping Beauty'.

Some have thought that this is the meaning of the universe. Kepler, inspired by pitagorean mysticism, wanted to hear the silent music which was being played by the divine composer, stars and planets being the instruments. If he looked for the mathematical regularities of the movements of the celestial bodies it was because he believed this to be the key to the musical harmony of the cosmos. No wonder that he gave the title of *De Harmonice Mundi* to his great book on astronomy. He could repeat with the sacred poet: 'Without speech or language or sound of any voice, their music goes through all the earth' (Ps. 19.3–4), It is only in the human heart that God's perpetual fugue can be heard. We know it 'by heart'. We hear it because it is already written in our flesh. 'Even if the world outside disappeared,' remarks Hermann Hesse, 'any one of us would be able to recreate it, because mountains and rivers, trees and leaves, roots and flowers, all the forms which dwell in the world are pre-formed in us; they proceed from the soul, whose essence we ignore and whose existence is eternal and gives itself to us, above all as will to love and power to create – will and power which long for fulfilment' (*PLP* 141).

Others have heard the endless canon in the very structure of the organism. Merleau-Ponty, quoting the biologist Uexküll (who is also invoked by Ernst Cassirer, in the beginning of his anthropology), says that 'each organism is a melody which plays itself' (*SB* 159). Butterflies, snails, cicadas, ants, robins, squirrels: each of them is a unique form of beauty; out of their bodies different forms of music invade the spaces, looking for echoes and reverberations. Their hypothesis is that somewhere, outside, their sleeping beauty lies dormant, waiting for their kiss. And when the miracle occurs, when something responds to their call of beauty, a world is created, in the image and likeness of their own beauty. 'If plants had eyes, taste and judgement', says Feuerbach, 'each plant would declare its own flower the most beautiful. The life of an emphemera is extraordinarily short in comparison with that of longer-lived creatures; but, nevertheless, for the emphemera this short life is as long as a life of years to the others. The leaf on which the caterpillar lives is for it a world, an infinite space' (*EC* 8).

The myths of creation are another version of Narcissus' myth. God created the universe as a mirror where his/her/its beauty could be seen. The beauty that we see in the world is the beauty which abides in our bodies. Feuerbach was right: 'In the object we contemplate we become acquainted with ourselves' (*EC* 5). The universe is our mirror, we are God's mirror, we are the universe's mirror. 'Our body is a thinking mirror of the universe . . .' (*FP* 144).

Indeed, how could God create a Paradise if this garden of delights were not alive in her inexhaustible body. The garden is the visible image of the divine beauty. I remember Augustine's poem in his *Confessions*:

> I asked the earth,
> I asked the sea and the deeps,

among the living animals the things that creep.
I asked the winds that blow,
I asked the heavens, the sun, the moon, the stars,
and to all the things that stand at the doors of my flesh . . .
My question was the gaze I turned to them.
Their answer was their beauty . . . (C 234).

And yet, how marginal beauty has been in our theological meditations! Have we been afraid of the curse of narcissism? Have we separated goodness from beauty? Is this the reason why our theological discourse has been dominated by the ethical motif – the divine imperative – as opposed to the aesthetical – the divine delight? Agape against Eros? But is not the purpose of Agape the restoration of Eros, that the whole universe be loved *because of its beauty* and not *in spite of its ugliness*? The artist loves the formless stone because his eyes see the Pieta which lies dormant inside it. When Agape finishes his work, Eros explodes, triumphant. The ethical is not an end; it is only a means. The goal of all heroic struggles for the creation of a just and free world is the opening of spaces for the blossoming of the garden. Berdyaev was one of the few theologians to understand the metaphysical meaning of beauty. He says:

Beauty is a characteristic of a higher qualitative condition of being, of a higher attainment of existence, rather than a separate phase of existence. We may say that beauty is not only an aesthetic category, but a metaphysical category, as well. If man receives anything into himself integrally, it is beauty. We say 'what a beautiful spirit, a beautiful life, a beautiful action, etc.' This is not only an aesthetic evaluation, it is an integral evaluation. Everything harmonic in our life is beauty . . . Beauty is the final purpose of human life and the life of the world. Good is a means, a way, and it arose in opposition to evil (the knowledge of good and evil). Beauty lies beyond the knowledge of good and evil. But the good which lies beyond the distinction between good and evil where evil is forgotten, is also beauty. In beauty there can

[127]

never be that moral distortion which characterizes evil. The beauty of evil is illusion and deceit. We can think of the Kingdom of God only as the kingdom of beauty. The transfiguration of the world is a phenomenon of beauty. *And all the beauty in the world is either a remembrance of paradise or a prophecy of a transfigured world* (CE 319).

Salvation is the recovery of the polyphony of life. It is Bonhoeffer who says it. And it is revealing and moving to realize that this image came to his mind when his death was already foreseeable, when nothing else could be done, when all ethical and political hopes had gone, when he was alone, before the abyss. These are his words, in a letter of May 20th, 1944:

> There is always a danger of intense love destroying what I might call the 'polyphony' of life. What I mean is that God requires that we should love him eternally with our whole hearts, yet not so as to compromise or diminish our earthly affections, but as a kind of *cantus firmus* to which the other melodies of life provide the counterpoint. Where the ground bass is firm and clear, there is nothing to stop the counterpoint from being developed to the utmost of its limits. Both ground bass and counterpoint are 'without confusion and yet distinct', in the words of the Chalcedonian formula, like Christ in his divine and human natures. Perhaps the importance of polyphony in music lies in the fact that it is a musical reflection of this Christological truth, and that it is therefore an essential element in the Christian life. Only a polyphony of this kind can give life a wholeness, and at the same time assure us that nothing can go wrong so long as the *cantus firmus* is kept going. Please do not fear or hate separation, if it should come . . . Pin your faith in the *cantus firmus* . . . (PFG 131–132).

Gaston Bachelard, as we already mentioned, speaks about the 'fundamental dreams', and remarks that the only way to convince is by bringing them back to memory (*DS* xxiv). I believe that

Paradise is our original fundamental dream, and that once we see it we also hear the *cantus firmus* which it plays.

> These tall trees
> are like green harps
> with its rain-strings
> plucked by the wind.
>
> The clearest sounds come
> from the yellow almond-tree,
> all spotted in the palms
> of its tough, verdant leaves.
>
> The most fragile sounds
> are born in the acacia foliage,
> with fluffy bunches of flowers
> and little parallel leaves.
>
> The gravest sounds roll
> down the old, black mangoes
> with thick, twisted branches
> and parasites for fringes.
>
> And sounds remotest and vaguest
> come from slender cypresses,
> they come and are quenched in mist,
> they are sketched and vanish . . . (*VRE* 41).

We were born in a garden, there is a garden inside our bodies, and we are destined by divine vocation to be gardeners, because God also is a gardener. God was not happy in the infinity of the universe. His work moves from the boundless lifeless spaces of the universe to this little, circumscribed space, where life makes love with beauty. In the garden his work is finished. In the garden he finds pleasure. He rests from work. He becomes, then, pure contemplation, pure play, pure enjoyment. Nothing else is to be done. No ethics, no commandment, no politics: there is a fruit to be eaten.

As opposed to the scientists who look for the most abstract, God gives birth to the most concrete. It is in the concreteness of beauty that God's universality is revealed. The verses, again, are from Cecília Meireles:

> In the mystery of the Never-Ending
> balances a planet.
> And, on the planet, a garden,
> and, in the garden, a flower-bed;
> and in the flower-bed, a violet,
> and all day long, above the violet,
> between the planet and the Never-Ending,
> a butterfly's wing (*VRE* 21).

Paradise is the mystery of Creation and Incarnation in sensuous form.

> Sursum corda! Lift up your souls, says Álvaro de Campos.
> Matter, the whole matter, is Spirit!
> O Earth, suspended garden . . . (*P* 105–106).

Paradise: God's entrails given not to thought – as theologians like to do – but given to be eaten. Theology as poetic gardening . . .

Artists have known this all the time, regardless of the material means they use to materialize their dream. 'The Universe', says Bachelard, commenting on Chagall's drawings – 'beyond all its miseries, has a destiny of happiness. We must reencounter Paradise' (*DS* 21).

You remember that I compared the body to a palympsest. What is written in our flesh, with invisible characters, is the memory and prophecy of Paradise.

The desert is beautiful because it hides, somewhere, a garden.

We are beautiful because inside us there is a garden which, once in a while, let's itself to be seen through our gestures.

Paradise is the supreme metaphor of our bodies, a place of pure delight. The lover says:

My bride is a garden (Songs of Songs 4.12).

And the prophet repeats:

You will be like well-watered gardens (Isa. 58.11).

As the purpose of God's work, in the six days of creation, was the planting of Paradise, so the purpose of everything we do, from play to politics, is the recovery of the lost garden. Both in the body of a child and in the body of the warrior lives the same dream. And unless we remember this dream, we are condemned to be unhappy. What psychoanalysis does is simply to re-state what prophets and mystics have been saying. 'It is the human ego that carries the search for a world to love', says Norman O. Brown. 'Or rather, this project, in the unconscious stratum of the ego, guides human consciousness in its restless search for an object that can satisfy its love' (*LAD* 46). As Angelus Silesius once said in a verse,

> Unless you find Paradise
> at your center,
> there is not the smallest chance
> that you may enter (*BAS* 31).

To plant a little garden is easy. My body has power enough to do it. As I enjoy my little garden I eat a sacrament, a fragment of the great garden. But this little space is not enough to satisfy my hunger for joy. We are unhappy because we cannot eat all that we see. The whole universe must be served as a messianic banquet. But this task is too big for me. It demands many bodies, many gardeners. The re-creation of Paradise demands the dreams and work of a whole people. And this is politics. Even Marx, in that moment of poetic inspiration, recognized that inside the body of a warrior there must be the hope of a living flower to be culled. Inside the body of the Lion, says Zarathustra in his parable, there lives a Child, who wants to play. Every creator must become an enjoyer. The purpose of war is the end of all wars, the purpose of work is the end of work: struggle is fulfilled in beauty. And we

[131]

return to the wisdom of the Old Testament way of counting time. The Christians transformed the day of enjoyment in a preparation for work. It comes at the beginning. But the Old Testament reverses this order: work exists for the purpose of enjoyment.

But the Devil never rests. It is right in Paradise that his words are heard, as if he belonged there. 'Beauty has its own dialectics', says Berdyaev, 'and Dostoievski has something to say about it. He thought that beauty would save the world. But he also says: "Beauty is not only a terrible but a mysterious thing. Here the devil struggles with God, and the battlefield is the human heart." The devil wants to use beauty for his own end' (*CE* 319–320).

Beauty has its place in the human heart, which is the centre of the body. The body is the instrument which sings it.

The Blacks in Brazil brought from Africa a musical instrument called 'berimbau': one single string, stretched between the two ends of a tensed bow. The player varies the tension of the bow and hits the string with a metal piece. And thus music is produced. And they dance . . .

Our body, a berimbau: a string tensed by a bow.

The string is Life, Eros.

The bow is Death, Thanatos.

Out of the marriage between Life and Death beauty is born. This is why it is always mixed with a bit of sadness. Even gardens know winters. There is a tragic element in beauty. What Wordsworth said about the beauty of a sunset can also be said of all works of art.

> The clouds that gather round the setting sun
> do take a sober colouring from an eye that
> has kept watch o'er man's mortality (*SNL* 20).

The sunset is beautiful because it is a metaphor of ourselves. We are rainbows just before darkness, playing colours before night arrives. Even the lightest of Mozart's sonatas has the same drop of sadness, because sooner or later the final chord will be played. And there will be silence and nostalgia before the 'no longer'.

Beauty is life's triumph over death. It is life's melody as it faces the Abyss. 'Beauty', says Rilke, 'is the Terrible that we bear and admire, and yet we are not destroyed by it' (*ED 3*).

Beauty makes use of the Enemy. It transforms Death into a friend. The bow does not break the string. It makes it possible for the string to sing a melody. And the miracle happens. In Rilke's words again, the body is then capable of 'holding Death, the whole of Death, sweetly, without becoming evil . . .' (*ED 24*). And the *cantus firmus* is heard . . .

But the Adversary, the Devil, the Tester, also likes to play with the berimbau. But he does not want the *cantus firmus* to be heard. He wants to break the string.

The human heart becomes the battle field between God and the Devil. And it is as if the two of them were accomplices in the same game. God allows the Tester to tense the bow to its utmost limits. God bets that Eros will triumph. But the Devil bets on Death.

> The time came when God put Abraham to the test (Gen. 22.1).

'Abraham, Abraham, I have been hearing your *cantus firmus*, and it is beautiful. Indeed, you have reasons to be joyful. It is not surprising that this beauty grows out of your old body. You have Isaac. You are beautiful *because of* Isaac. But I wonder: Will you continue to sing the same song if Isaac dies? Take your son, your only son, whom you love, and offer him as a sacrifice . . .' (Gen. 22.2). And when these words were heard, God took on the form of a Devil in Abraham's eyes. The moment of the test had arrived. He would have to play his *cantus firmus* facing the Abyss.

And the time came when God allowed Job to be put through the test. 'The day came when the members of the court of heaven took their places in the presence of the Lord, and Satan, the Adversary, was among them. Then the Lord said to Satan: "Have you seen my servant Job? Have you heard this melody? Is there anything more beautiful than it, in the whole world?" Satan answered the Lord: "Indeed, his music is beautiful. But with good reasons. You have granted him all good things of life. But hold the bow of death! Stretch its string to its limits. You will see that it is weak. It will break . . .' And Job was put to the test: but even without its instrument, his *cantus firmus* was heard in the wilderness . . .

And Jesus was lead by the Spirit to the desert, to be put to the proof by the devil (Matt. 4.1).

'Do you believe that it is a beautiful thing to be a man? This is the melody I hear, coming from your body and soul. But to be a man is to live tensed by death. How could you hold death inside you, sweetly, without becoming evil? See how thin and weak you are! Death is silently and slowly claiming to herself what she believes to be hers: your body. Don't you hear the noise of the gravediggers? Don't you hear the howling of the wolves? It is an impossible task to play Life when one is surrounded by Death! But this is what it means to be a human being! How could you save humankind from death if you yourself are doomed to die? Don't you see that the bow of Death will sooner or later break the string of love? Sing another melody. Instead of playing "man", why don't you play a safer melody: "God"? If you play "God" you will not have to face the Abyss . . .'

And our trembling bodies pray, as they face the terrible possibility: 'And don't bring us to the test' (Matt. 6.13).

If the string of Eros is weak, Death breaks it. The body is then no longer able to hold Death sweetly, without becoming evil. And the living ones are possessed by it.

> The hand of the Lord came upon me, and he carried me out by his Wind and put me down in a plain full of bones. He made me go to and fro across them until I had been round them all; they covered the plain, countless numbers of them, and they were very dry (Ezek. 37.1–2).

Gone is the hope that deserts will become gardens: the gardeners are dead. Gone is the hope that the *cantus firmus* will continue to be heard: the hands of the players are dry bones and there is no breath in their skeletons to blow their flutes . . .

> And the Lord God said to me: 'Man, can these bones live again?' I answered: Only thou knowest that . . . He said to me, 'Prophesy over these bones . . . (Ezek. 37.3–4).

And a new song is heard, the song of the prophet, a song to ressurect the dead. The prophet 'stands in the middle of the crowd, but his roots are not in the crowd. He emerges according to broader laws. The future brutally speaks through him' (Rilke).

The prophet lives in the future. He sees the semblance of life which shines on the surface of the graveyard: too much talking, too much doing, eating and drinking before the flood, towers which are built to reach heavens. But he is an exile, he lives in a different time, his nest is built in the future. 'And in his solitude eagles shall bring him nourishment in their beaks. And he wants to live among men like strong winds, neighbors of the eagles, neighbors of the snow, neighbors of the sun . . . And like the wind he wants to blow among them' (*PN* 211).

> Then the Lord said to me: 'Prophesy to the Wind, prophesy, man, and say to it, These are the words, of the Lord God, O Wind, come from every quarter and breathe into these slain, that they may come to life . . . (Ezek. 37.9).

The poet plays his song to the living ones.

But when he sings his song to the dead, he becomes a prophet. He sings because he believes that Eros is eternal. It never dies . . . Eros lives eternally as dreams. He believes that 'life's splendour forever lives in wait about each one of us in all its fullness, but veiled from view, deep down, invisible, far off. It is there, though not hostile, not reluctant, not deaf. If you summons it by the right word, by its right name, it will come. This is the essence of magic, which does not create but summons' (Quoted by Skip Strickland, mimeographed paper, 'A theology and brief story of clowning from my perspective').

Which word if this, which has the power to invoke the Wind and to resurrect the dead?

His is not a lament song. The prophet subverts the funeral.

The Devil plays the funeral march with his bow and broken string.

The prophet hums a lullaby.

The body has grown old and the blood of fertility has ceased to visit his wife for long. And yet he builds a crib.

The city is surrounded by the armies of the enemy, and yet he takes all his savings and buys a piece of land . . .

'The girl is not dead', he says; 'she is asleep' (Matt. 9.24).

The prophet breaks the etiquette of death. He does not know how to dance her rhythms . . .

The prophet does not speak as a professor. Professors are committed to what is solid; the prophet invokes the Wind. Professors have mirrors in their hands. They are at the service of reality. They want to be faithful reflections of reality. But if the dead could see the face of their own death reflected in a mirror, they would die a second death.

The prophet is not a painter, either. He does not cover the dead bodies with the colours of the rainbow. He does not romanticize death. He sees it as it is: ugly, in her full horror. 'The grave is eternity, death is life, the ugly is beautiful': thus say the preachers of death, the false prophets, and their shrines are found all over the world. In some of them the dry bones are dressed with the glittering uniforms of heroes, those who died for the country, and the bodies of the living ones tremble as they hear the beat of the drums. Other shrines have the name of churches, and among them the Christian churches have become notable for the beauty of their aesthetics of death that they have developed. And the believers sing: the body must be denied for the soul to live.

But the prophet loves life. In his soul there lives a child. And, as we know, children don't like burials. They would rather play in the gardens. The prophet knows that we and God are destined to Paradise. How could he find happiness in heaven? We know that hell is unbearable. But, do we realize that heaven is unbearable also? Eliot speaks as a prophet when he says that we must be protected both from 'heaven and damnation which flesh cannot endure' (*CPP* 119).

The prophet does not speak about the immortality of the soul. He hopes for the resurrection of the body.

The prophet does not utter a divine imperative. One cannot command a stone to fly. How could the dead be commanded to come back to life?

The prophet is not a political leader, either. He stands at the end of politics, when nothing else can be done. His actions are not political actions. They are not *means* to certain ends. The prophetic word is a reversal of politics. No wonder he is laughed at (Matt. 9.24).

The prophet invokes the Wind. He calls the untamable. There are no birds in his cages, no swords in his hands, no wisdom in his mouth. He is empty, like the dead man. He speaks and hopes that the Wind will come, to resurrect the dead.

Albert Camus, in *The Myth of Sisyphus*, says that 'there is but one truly philosophical problem, and that is suicide. Judging whether life is or is not worth living amounts to answering the fundamental question of philosophy' (*MS* 3). I want to suggest that there is but one truly theological problem, and that is the resurrection of the dead.

The word which resurrects the dead: where does it come from?

Three centuries ago the Catholic preacher Antônio Vieira thus described the birth of the prophetic word:

> The words of those who did not see are mere words; but the words of those who saw are prophecies.
>
> The Ancient, when they wanted to foretell the future, sacrificed animals and consulted their entrails. According to what they saw in them, thus they prognosticated. They did not consult the head, which is the seat of the understanding; they consulted the entrails, which are the seat of love. Because those who better prognosticate are not those who better understand but rather those who love most. This usage was widespread all over Europe before the coming of Christ. And the Portuguese, among all other Gentiles, were peculiar in it. The others consulted the entrails of animals.

The Portuguese consulted the entrails of men. The superstition was false, but the allegory was very true. There is no surer light of prophecy than the one which is found in the entrails of men. Of whose men? Of all? No. Of those who have been sacrificed. If you want to prophecy futures, consult the entrails of those who were sacrificed, of those who sacrifice themselves. And whatever they say, this must be taken as prophecy. However, to consult those who did not, do not want and will not become sacrifices, is not to be willing to see true prophecies. It is to make the present blind and not to see the future (*ICB* xvii).

The prophetic word does not come out of the head.

The head is impotent to make love with the body.

It is not addressed to the head, either. Because the body abides in the depths inside the dark waters of the lake.

The prophet says what is written in the entrails of the slain. Dreams which were aborted by death. They are not dead. They only flew to the future, as fugitive birds . . .

The eucharist: a meal: bread and wine: the entrails of the Victim, offered as food and drink.

For centuries this story has been used to explain the mode of Christ's presence. But the eucharist does not explain a presence; it opens the wound of an Absence.

'Do this in remembrance of me . . .'

The Victim is still present. Very soon he will no longer be.

'Everything in him was a presence which stayed a little longer, a farewell ready to be accomplished . . .' (*FP* 145). The Tester tenses the bow of Thanatos to its utmost limits. But the string of Eros does not break. It continues to play the *cantus firmus* . . . Body and soul hold Death, the whole of Death, sweetly, without becoming evil. Death can be overcome. Before the Abyss, the memory of Paradise and the prophecy of a transfigured world. Memory and hope are born out of the entrails of the Victim, as a new-born baby . . .

The prophet eats the entrails of the Victim.

The dialectics of the prophetic word is the dialectic of eating: one eats and one is eaten. One is possessed by the Wind which dwells in the food. The prophet dreams the dreams of the Victim and speaks in tongues: an unknown language which all understand.

Pentecost.

The etiquette of Death is broken.

It is as if all were drunk . . .

The prophet stands at the end of the world. Death follows him, at the reach of his hand . . . He is before the Abyss, like the spider.

But he is also at the beginning of the world, facing chaos and darkness. One must be dead and buried, one must go through the waters, as the dead man – baptism – in order to be born again, out of the power Wind . . . One is alive only when one holds Death, the whole of Death, sweetly, without becoming evil . . .

His are not words of knowledge. Knowledge demands clear and distinct ideas . . . Knowledge only exists when one walks firmly on solid ground. But the prophet floats loose in the air . . . He names the Nameless: God . . . He has no science . . . He knows no theo-logy. His words are, indeed, the end of any attempt to put the flight of the birds inside cages. His feet are, indeed, in the world of 'is'. But his dreams abide in the Absence . . . How could he know the flight of the birds or the ways of the Wind? 'The Wind blows where it wills; you hear the sound of it, but you do not know where it comes from or where it is going' (John 3.8). The words of the prophet are not science but invocations, prayers . . . 'Were he to describe the world just as it is and in his words there would be nothing but many lies and no truth' (Tolstoi). Were he to say only what is given to knowledge and he would only say death. The villagers would speak only about a corpse, nothing but a corpse. This is all what the smooth surface of the lake shows . . .

His words know nothing of the categorical imperative either. Death tells that there is nothing to be done. Life will not come back by the power of his works. The ethical man is afraid of the Abyss. He cannot move amidst the darkness of the woods and the darkness of the deep waters. He wants to dissolve the mystery and says that life is resolved in the clarity of praxis. He turns his back to the Void and makes believe that his cobweb is securely tied in the solid ground of duty. His ships don't sail into the endless sea; they remain anchored in shallow waters, where no shipwreck is possible. He closes his eyes to the mystery of his own Being.

But the prophet takes Death as his adviser and he 'enjoys the inner freedom from the practical desire' (*CPP* 119). Like a taoist master he knows that, for the right thing to happen, one must refrain from doing.

The prophet speaks not to the dead but to the Wind.

He names what he does not know, he says what he cannot do.

Before the Mystery: grace.

He enters the woods, he dives into the deep waters . . .

He invokes something which is beyond knowing and doing: God . . .

The only thing he has is a wound in his flesh: the pain of Desire: longing. Restless is his heart . . .

Inside the Void, a universe slowly makes itself visible: dreams. What is not . . . And they are beautiful: a Garden . . . The same Garden which lives in the entrails of the Victim. And they blow with the Wind, and in the graveyard, life appears. A flower in the desert. The secret of the messianic hope. Paul Tillich, in one of his sermons, tells the following story: 'In the Nuremburg war-crime trials a witness appeared who had lived for a time in a grave in a Jewish grave-yard. It was the only place he and many others could live, when in hiding after they had escaped the gas chamber. During this time he wrote poetry, and one of his poems was the description of a birth. In a grave nearby a young woman gave birth to a boy. The eighty-year-old gravedigger, wrapped in a linen shroud, assisted. When the new-born uttered his first cry, the old man prayed: "Great God, has Thou finally sent the Messiah to us? For who else than the Messiah Himself can be born in a grave?"' (*SF* 65).

Beauty is the name that we give to this mysterious event: when

Life, gentle and weak, sweet and with no evil in it, is born out of the grave.

The poet who wrote this poem was the prophet, before the valley of dry bones. And as his poem was read and heard, it is sure that the faces of the dead were illuminated by memories of Paradise and hopes of a transfigured world . . .

And then, after that gust of Wind has blown on one's face, one returns from the edge of the cliff. But everything is different. Now one knows that knowledge and intelligence are nothing but 'a shadow of beauty' (Cecília Meireles) and that the 'head is only the entrails of the heart' (*PN* 128). And one knows also that ethics and politics are only the movement of the body as it thinks and works for the creation of Paradise.

Before the Abyss, the beautiful dream, the beginning of the world. Everything else we do is nothing more and nothing less than the endless 'variations' on this basic theme: we are destined to happiness.

> And when we have built an altar
> to the invisible light,
> we may set thereon
> the little lights
> for which our bodily vision is made (*CPP* 114).

REFERENCES

Nunc adeamus bibliothecam, non illam quidem
multis instructam libris, sed exquisitis.

Erasmus

AL   Paz, Octávio, *O Arco e a Lira*, Rio de Janeiro, Nova Fronteira 1982

B   Prado, Adélia, *Bagagem*, Rio de Janeiro, Nova Fronteira 1979

BAS   Frank, Frederick, *The Book of Angelus Silesius*, Santa Fé, Bear & Co. 1985

C   Andrade, Carlos Drummond de, *Corpo*, Rio de Janeiro, Record 1984

CD   Freud, Sigmund, *Civilization and its Discontents*, New York, W. W. Norton 1962

CE   Berdyaev, Nicolai, *Christian Existentialism*, New York, Harper & Row 1965

CEH   Veyne, Paul, *Comment on Écrit l'Histoire*, Paris, Sueil 1971

CG   Augustine, Saint, *The City of God*, New York, The Modern Library 1950

CPP   Eliot, T. S., *The Complete Poems and Plays*, New York, Harcourt, Brace & World and London, Faber & Faber 1971

CUP   Kierkegaard, Soren, *Concluding Unscientific Postscript*, Princeton, Princeton University Press 1962

DEBC   Kent, Corita (or.), *Damn Everything But the Circus*, New York, Holt, Rinehart & Winston 1970

DS   Bachelard, Gaston, *O Direito de Sonhar*, São Paulo, Difel 1985

EC   Feuerbach, Ludwig, *The Essence of Christianity*, New York, Harper & Row 1957

ED   Rilke, Reiner Maria *Elegias de Duino*, Porto Alegre, Globo 1972

EPP   Fairbairn, W. Ronald D., *Estudos Psicanalíticos da Personalidade*, Rio de Janeiro, Interamericana 1978

ER   Barth, Karl, *The Epistle to the Romans*, London, Oxford University Press 1933

FH   Dickinson, Emily, *Final Harvest*, Boston, Little, Brown & Co. 1961

FLW   Schmemann, Alexander, *For the Life of the World*, New York, NSCF 1963

FP   Meireles, Cecília, *Flor de Poemas*, Rio de Janeiro, Aguilar 1972.

FUS   Neurath, Otto (ed.), *Foundations of the Unity of Sciences*, Chicago, The University of Chicago Press 1971

FTM   Govinda, A., *Foundations of Tibetan Mysticism*, New York, 226, quoted in *LB 266*

GIP   Freud, Sigmund, *A General Introduction to Psychoanalysis* in *The Great Books of the Western World*, Chicago, London, Encyclopaedia Britannica 1971

GSV   Rosa, João Guimarães, *Grande Sertão-Veredas*, Rio de Janeiro, José Olympio 1978

ICB   Mota, Carlos Guilherme, *Ideologia da Cultura Brasileira*, São Paulo, Ática 1977

ILS   Kundera, Milan, *A Insutentável Leveza do Ser*, Rio de Janeiro, Nova Fronteira 1983

IS   Berger, Peter, *Invitation to Sociology*, Garden City, Doubleday 1963

IT   Buber, Martin, *I and Thou*, Edinburgh, T. & T. Clark 1955

IU   Mannheim, Karl, *Ideologia e Utopia*, Rio de Janeiro, Globo 1954

JI   Castañeda, Carlos, *Journey to Ixtlan*, New York, Simon & Schuster 1972

L   Barthes, Roland, *Leçon*, Paris, Sueil 1978

LAD   Brown, Norman O., *Life against Death*, New York, Random House 1959

LB   Brown, Norman O., *Love's Body*, New York, Vintage Books 1966

LSD   Popper Karl, *The Logic of Scientific Discovery*, New York, Harper & Row 1968

LV   Rosa, João Guimarães, 'Literatura e Vida', in *Arte em Revista*, São Paulo, Ceac 1983, ano I, n. 2

M   Descartes, René, *Meditations*, in *The Great Books of the Western World* vol. 31

MCM   Fromm, Erich, *Marx's Concept of Man*, New York, Frederick Ungar 1964

MEPP   Anon., *Modern Etiquette in Private and Public*, Frederick Warne 1872. Transcribed in Douglas, Mary (ed.), *Rules and Meanings*, Harmondsworth, Penguin Books 1973

MHO   Bloch, Ernst, *Man on His Own*, New York, Herder & Herder 1970

MK   Hermann, Fabio, *Melanie Klein*, São Paulo, Ática 1972

MS   Camus, Albert, *The Myth of Sysiphus*, New York, Vintage Books 1965

MSR   Malinowski, Bronislaw, *Magic, Science and Religion*, Garden City, Doubleday 1954

MW   Gerth & Mills (ed.), *From Max Weber*, New York, Oxford Press 1964

O   Valéry, Paul, *Oeuvres*, Paris, Bibliotheque de la Pleiade, vol. 1

OCD   Augustine, Saint, *On Christian Doctrine*, Indianapolis, Bobbs Merrill 1958

ODP   Freud, Sigmund, *The Origin and Development of Psychoanalysis* in *The Great Books of the Western World*, vol. 51

OoR   Rosenstock-Huessy, Eugen, *Out of Revolution*, New York, Four Wells 1964

OR   Marx and Engels, *On Religion*, New York, Schocken 1964

PAC   Campos, Álvaro de (Fernando Pessoa), *Poesias de Álvaro de Campos* Lisboa, Ática 1978

PAlbC   Caeiro, Alberto (Fernando Pessoa), *Poemas de Alberto Caeiro*, Lisboa Ática 1979

PB   Blake, William, *The Portable Blake*, New York, Viking Press 1979

PE   Weber, Max, *The Protestant Ethic and the Spirit of Capitalism*, New York, Scribner's 1958

PF   Bloch, Ernst, *A Philosophy of the Future*, New York, Herder & Herder 1963

PFG   Bonhoeffer, Dietrich, *Prisoner for God*, New York Macmillan 1954

PFP   Pessoa, Fernando, *Poesias de Fernando Pessoa*, Lisboa, Ática 1978

PLP   Hesse, Hermann, *Para Ler e Pensar*, Rio de Janeiro, Record 1971

PM   Hegel, G. W. F., *The Phenomenology of the Mind*, New York, Harper & Row 1967

PN   Kaufman, Walter, *The Portable Nietzsche*, New York, The Viking Press 1965

R   Camus, Albert, *The Rebel*, New York, Vintage Books 1956

RD   Andrade, Carlos Drummond de, *Reunião*, Rio de Janeiro, José Olympio 1977

RR   Marcuse, Herbert, *Reason and Revolution*, Boston, Beacon Press 1960

SB   Merleau-Ponty, Maurice, *The Structure of Behavior*, Boston, Beacon Press 1967

SC   Berger, Peter, *The Sacred Canopy*, Garden City, Doubleday 1967

SF   Berdyaev, Nicolas, *Slavery and Freedom*, London, Geoffrey Bless 1943

SN   Borges, Jorge Luis, *Sete Noites*, São Paulo, Max Limonad 1983

SNL   Cummings, E. E., *Six Non-Lectures*, Cambridge, Harvard University Press 1953

SOF   Tillich, Paul, *The Shaking of the Foundations*, New York, Charles Scribner's Sons 1958

ST   Tillich, Paul, *Systematic Theology*, Chicago, The University of Chicago Press 1951

T   Rosa, João Guimarães, *Tutameia*, Rio de Janeiro, Nova Fronteira 1985

TLP   Wittgenstein, Ludwig, *Tractatus Logico-Philosophicus*, London, Routledge and Kegan Paul 1971

TR   Mendes, Murilo, *Transistor*, Rio de Janeiro, Nova Fronteira 1980

TTC   Lao Tsu, *Tao Te Ching*, New York, Vintage Books 1972

VAP   Moraes, Vinicius, *Antologia Poética*, Rio de Janeiro, José Olympio 1983

VRE   Meireles, Cecília, *Verdes Reinos Encantados*, Rio de Janeiro, Salamandra 1988 (Bi-lingual edition: Portuguese and English)

WWJC   Bonhoeffer, Dietrich, *Wer ist und wer war Jesus Christus*, Hamburg, Furche-Verlag 1962